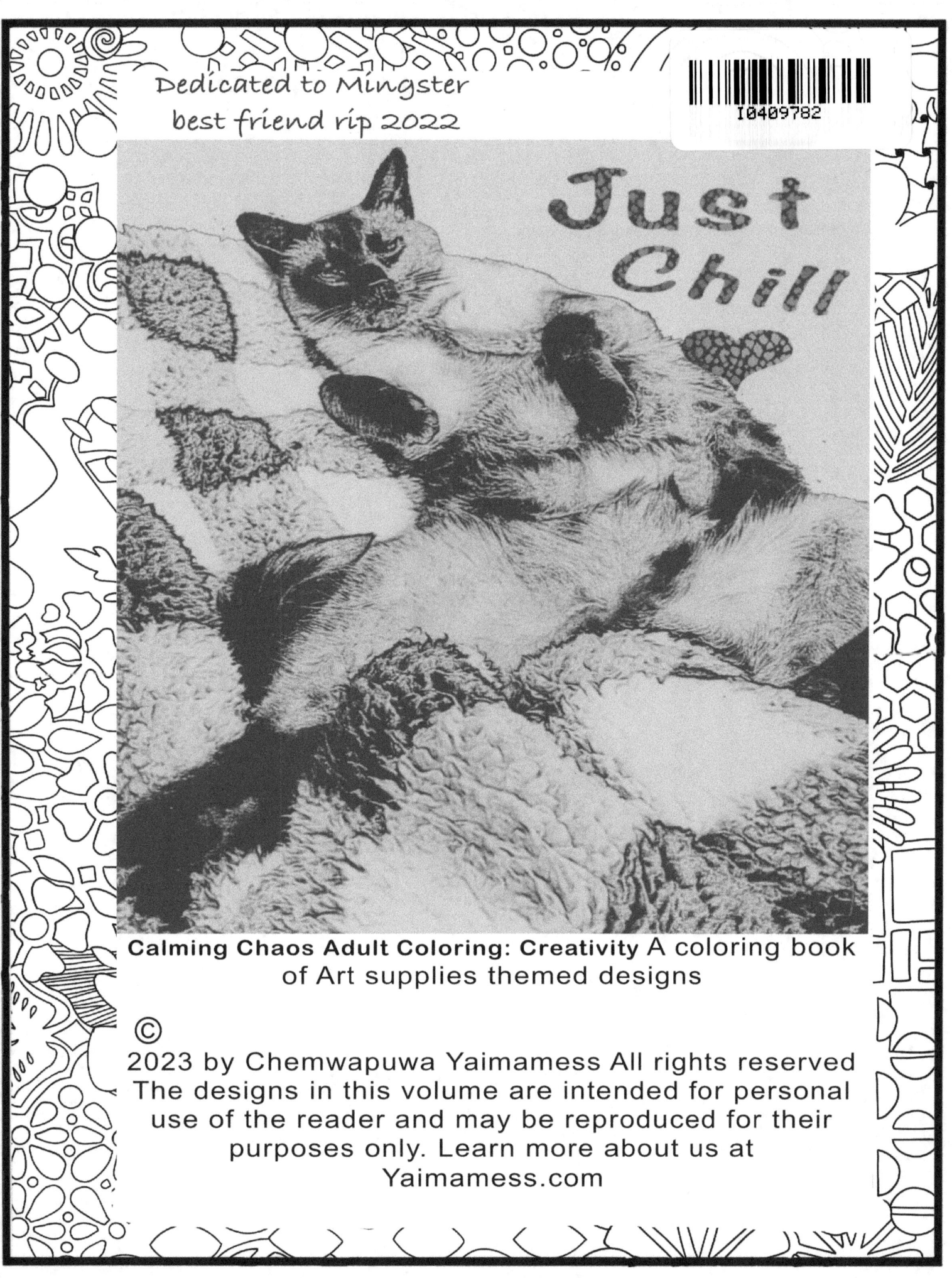

Dedicated to Mingster
best friend rip 2022

Just Chill

Calming Chaos Adult Coloring: Creativity A coloring book of Art supplies themed designs

This book belongs to:

_____

_____

_____

_____

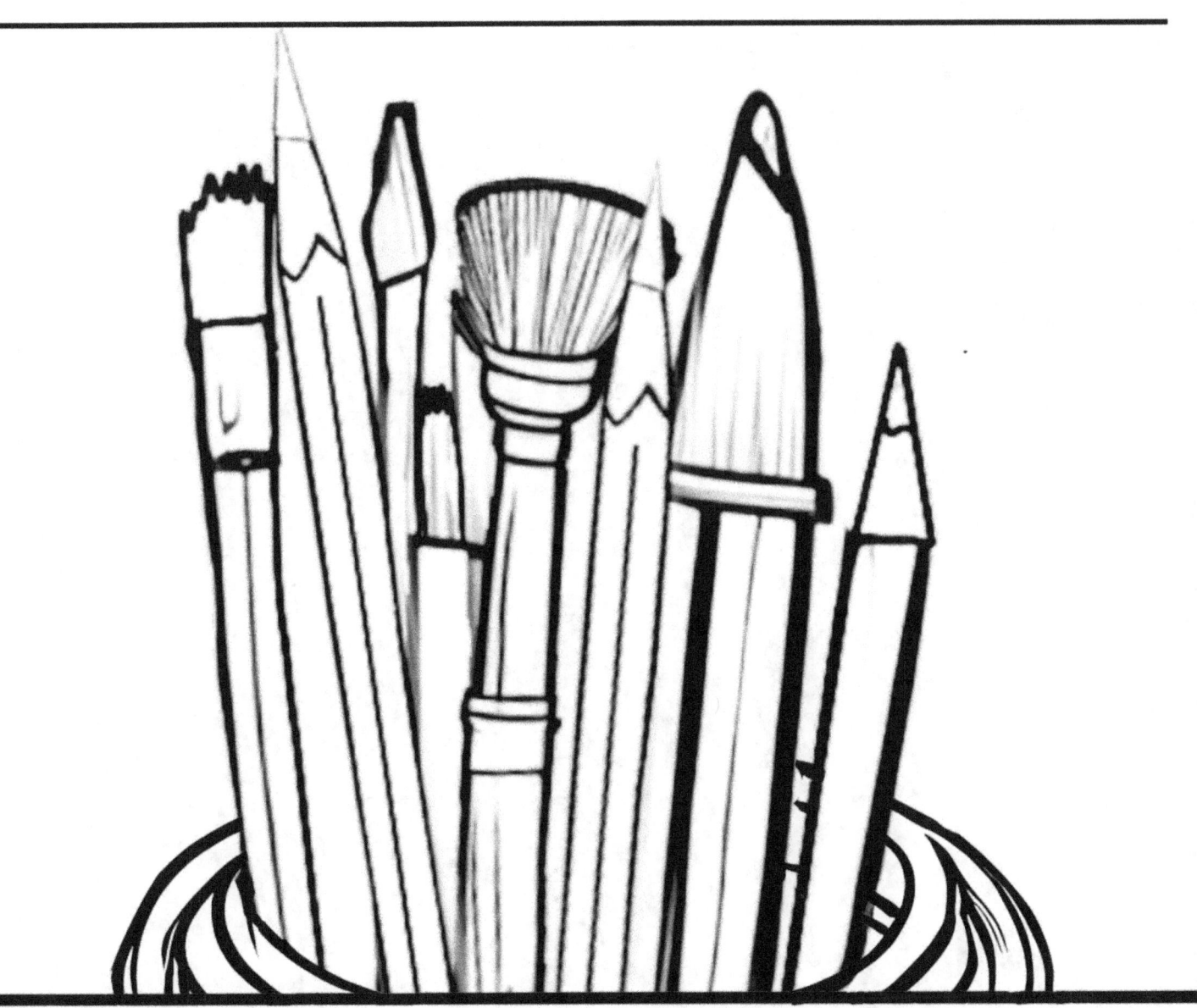

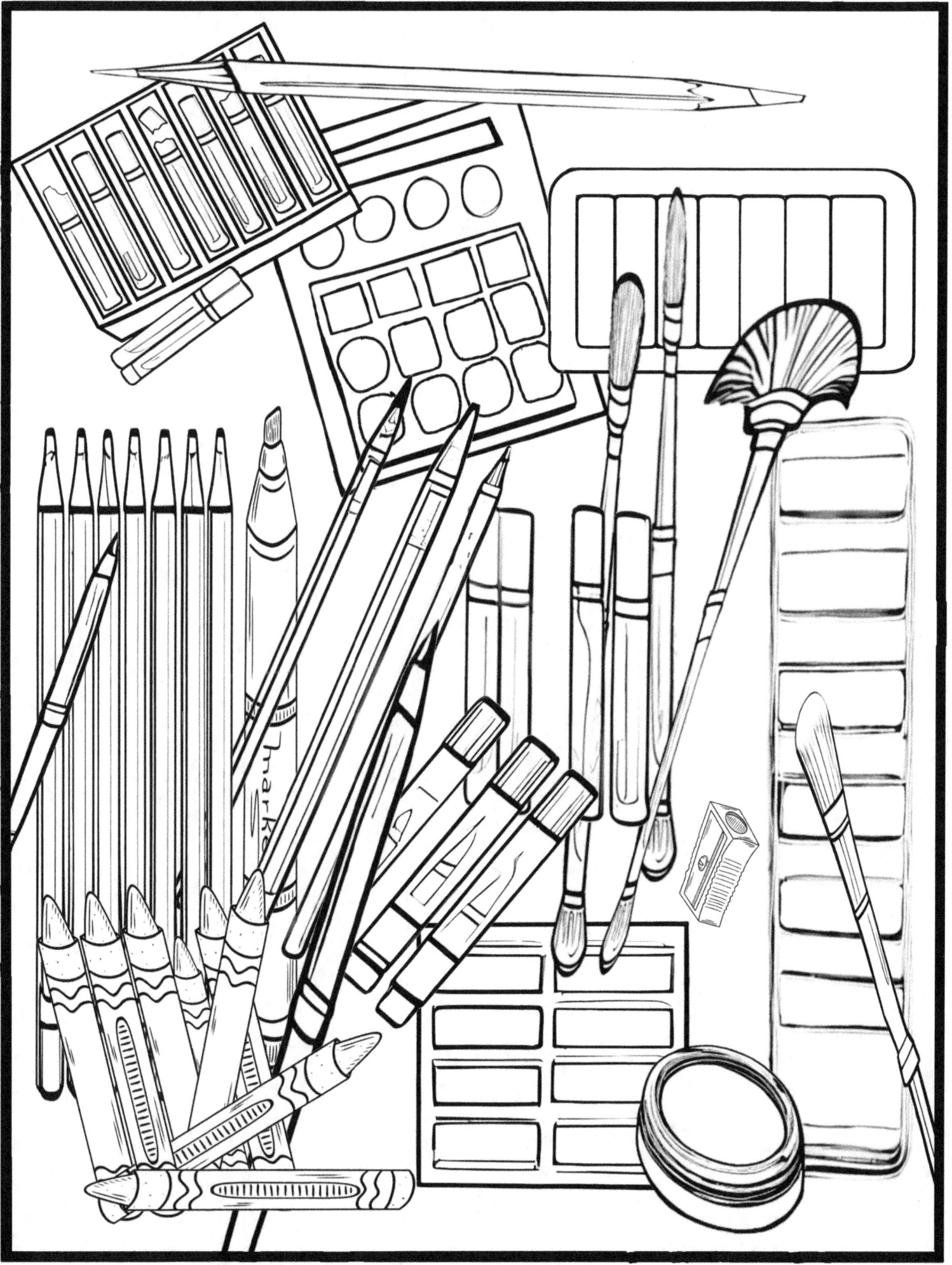

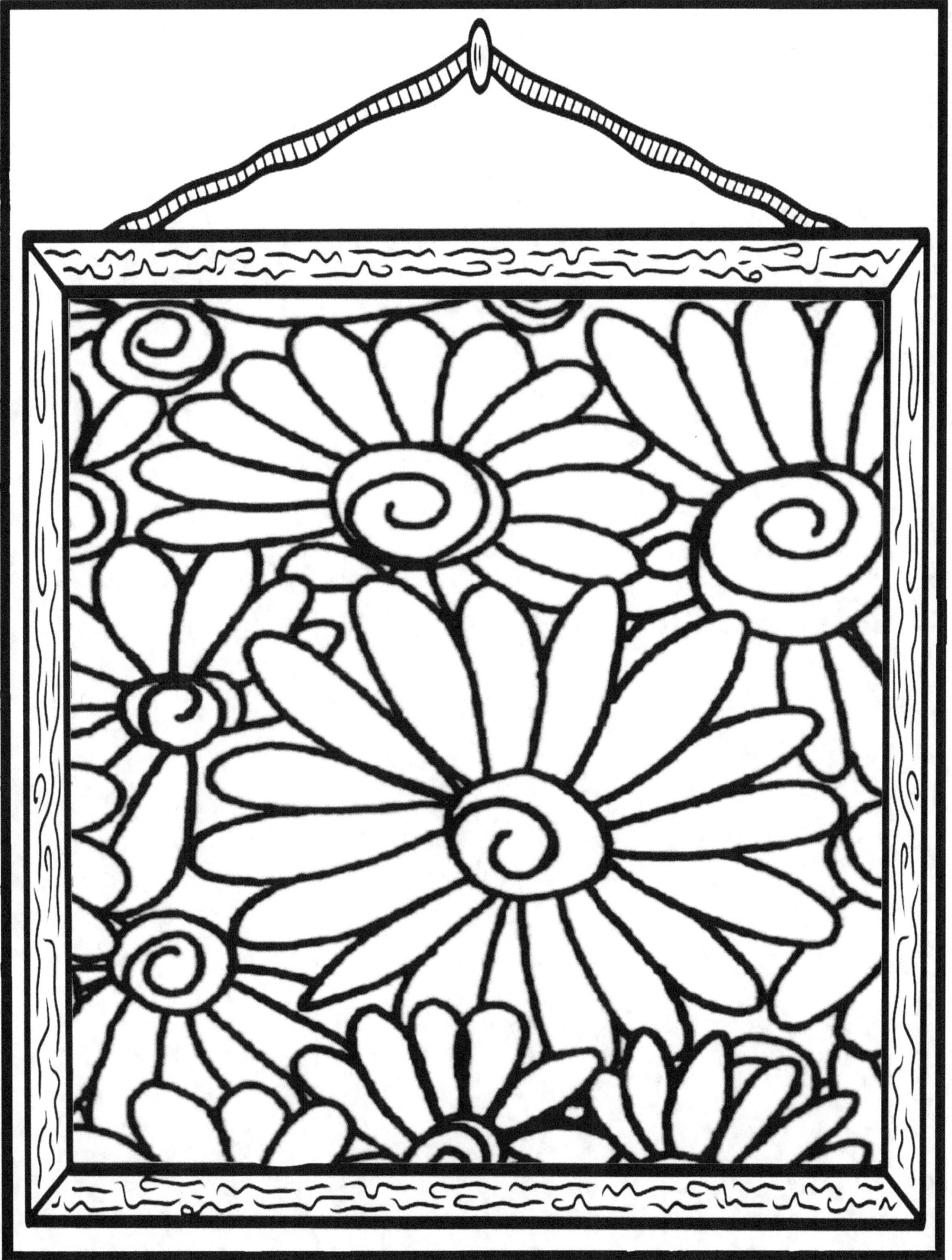

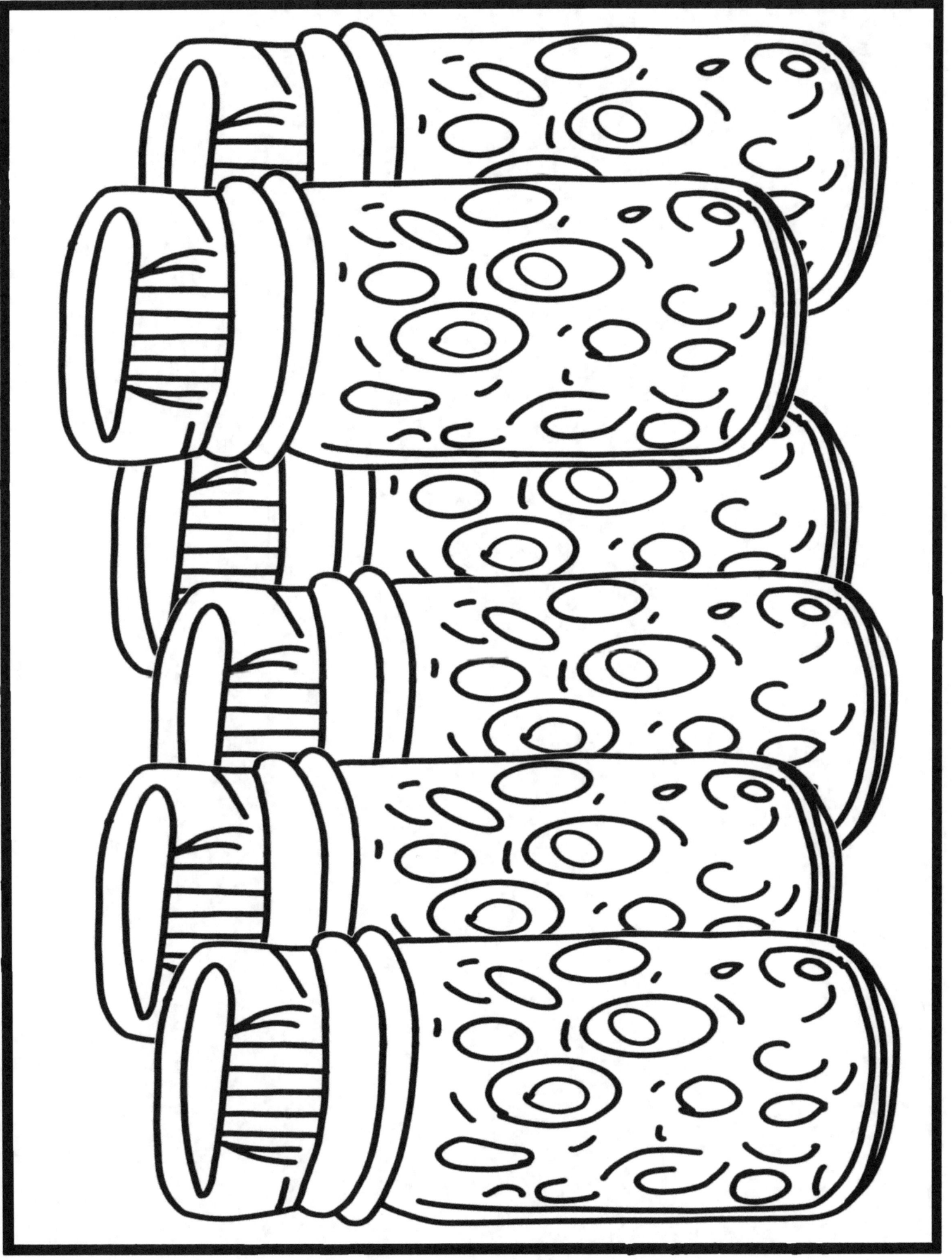

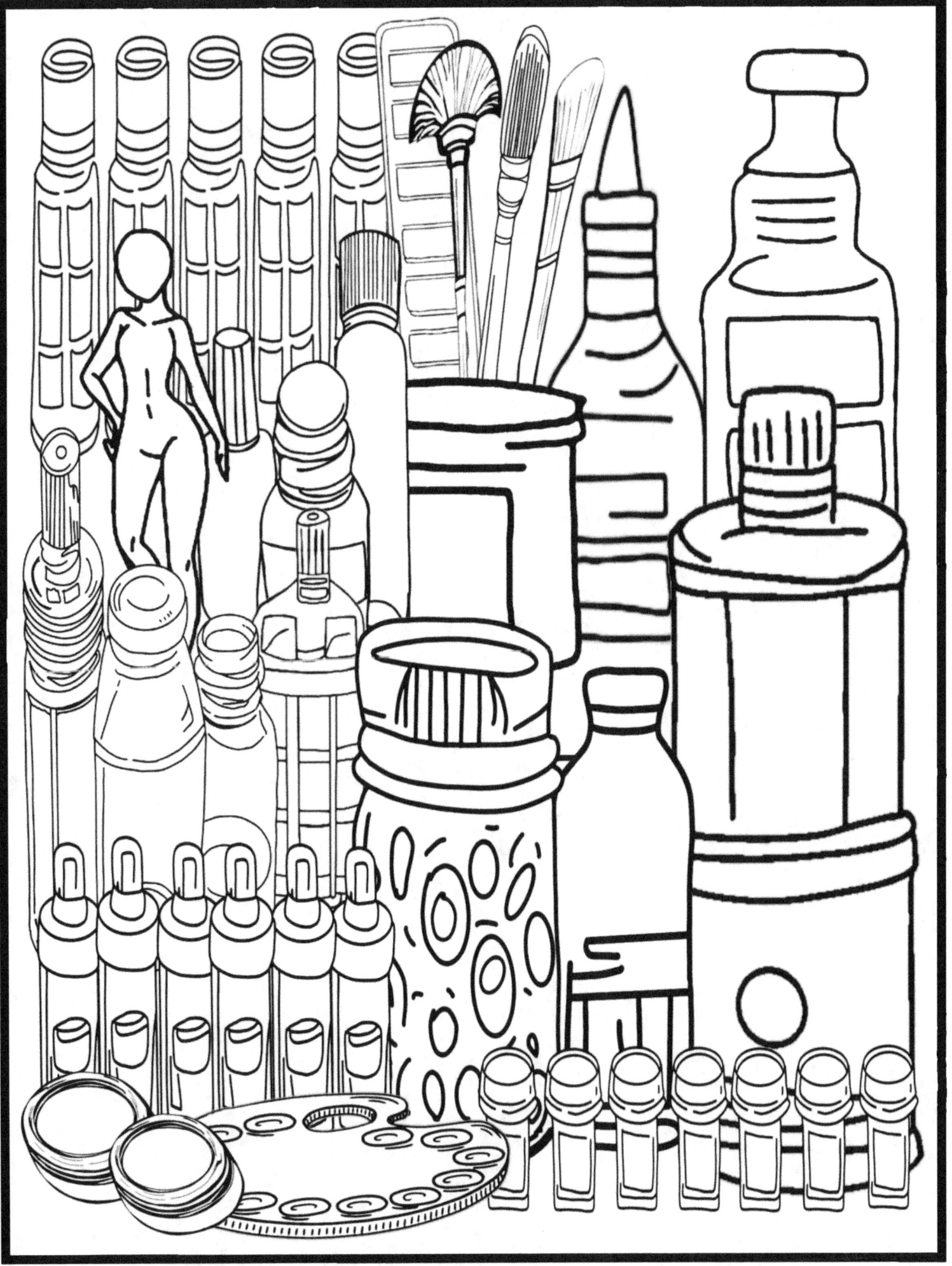

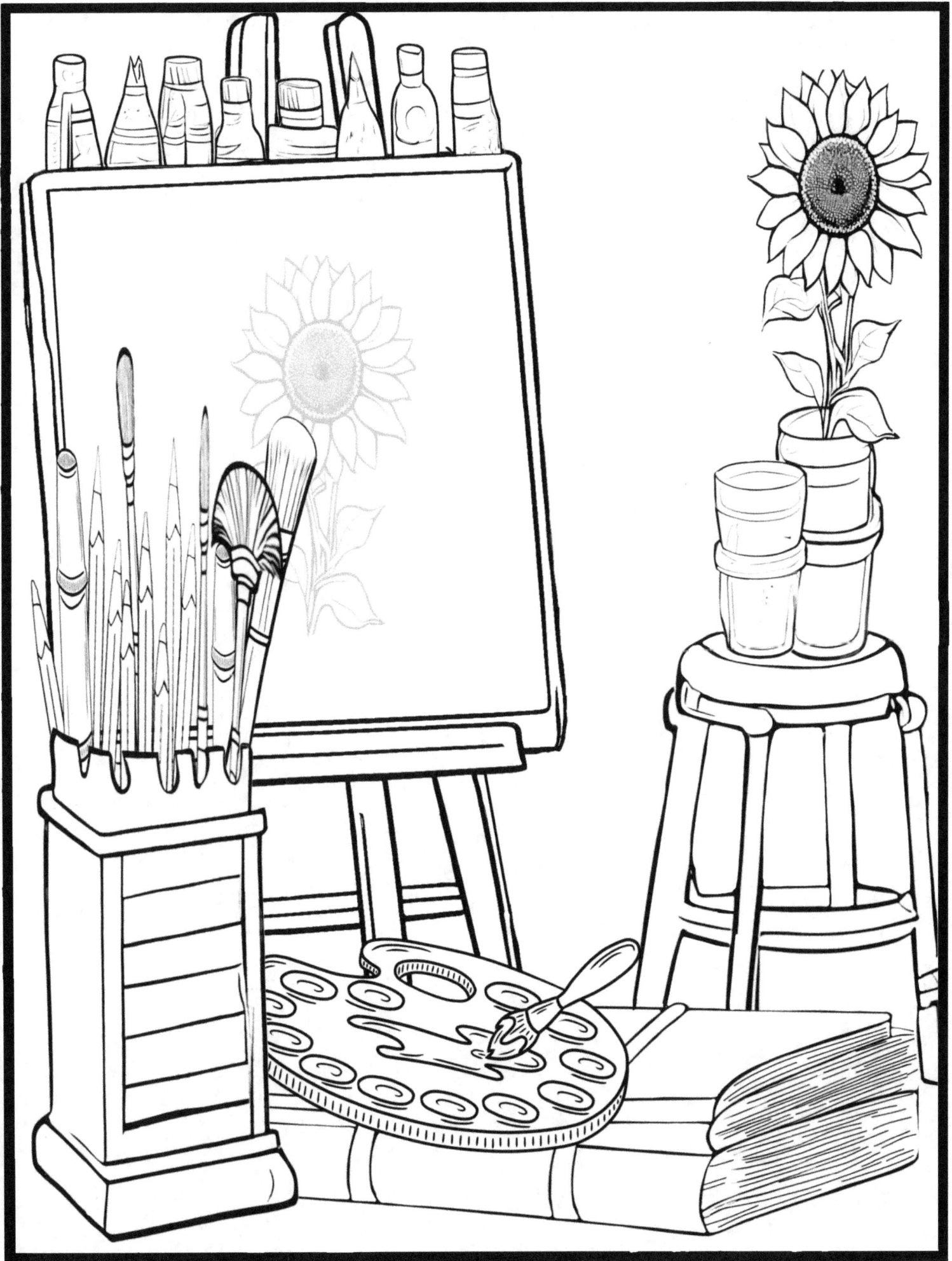

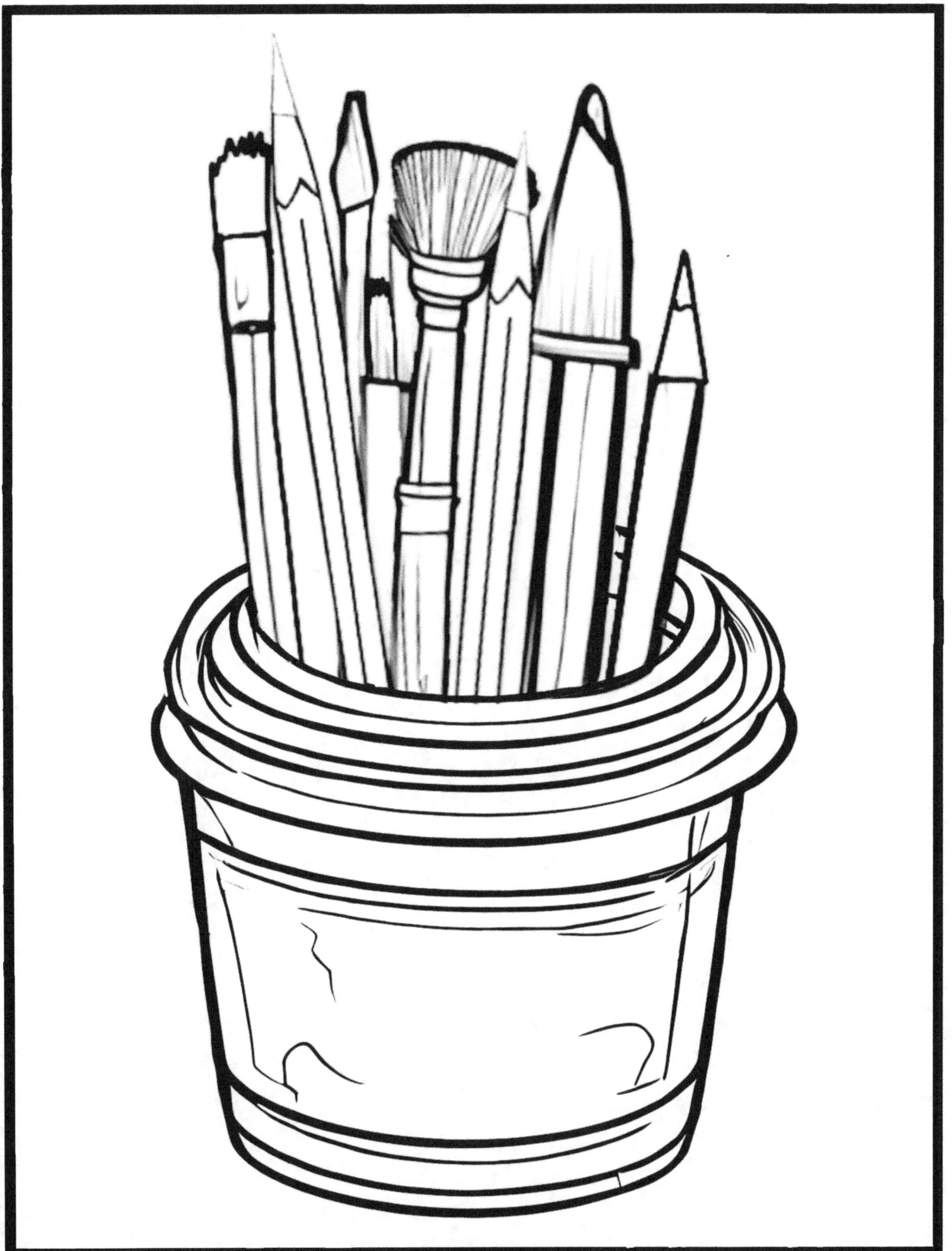

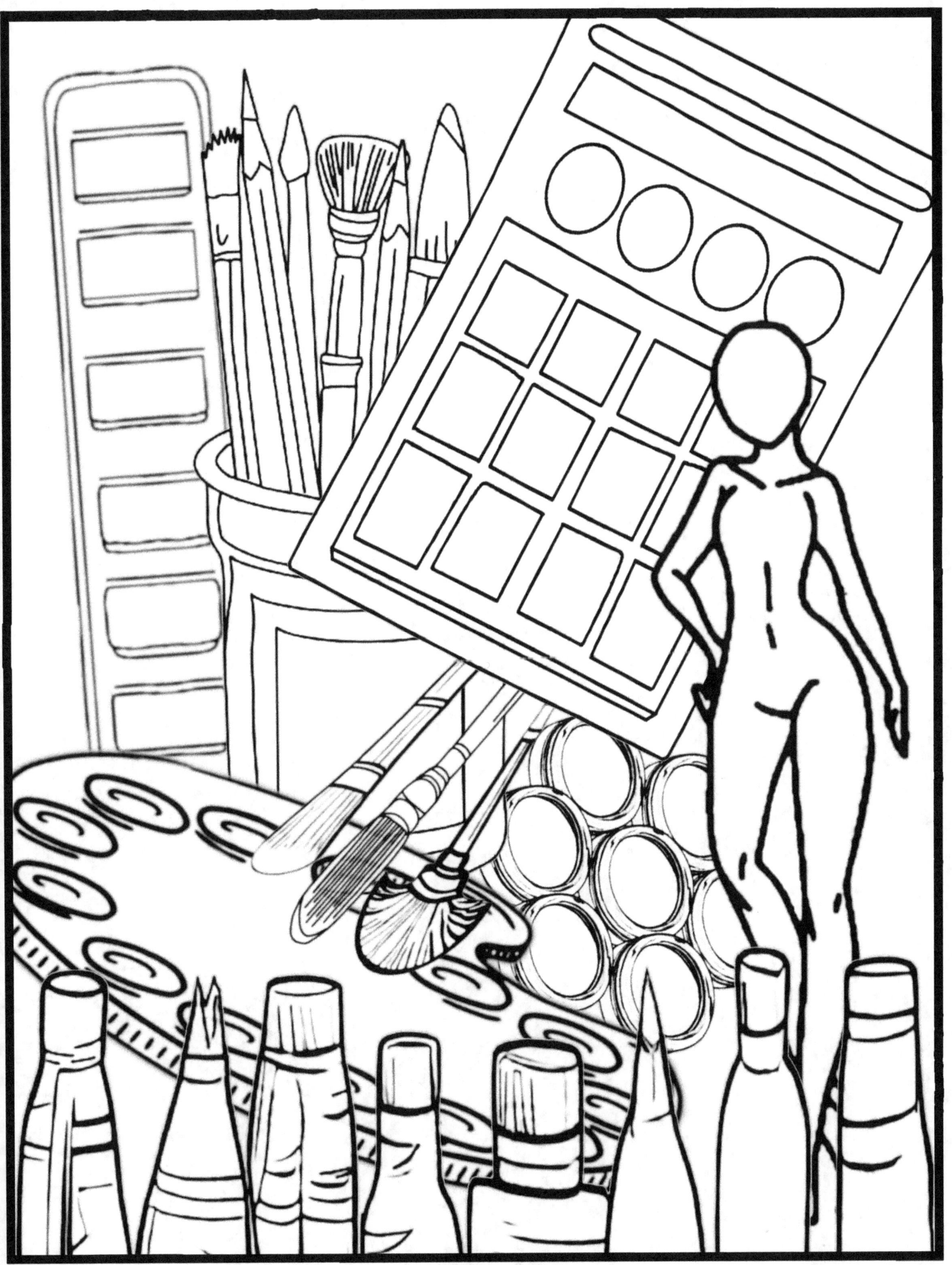

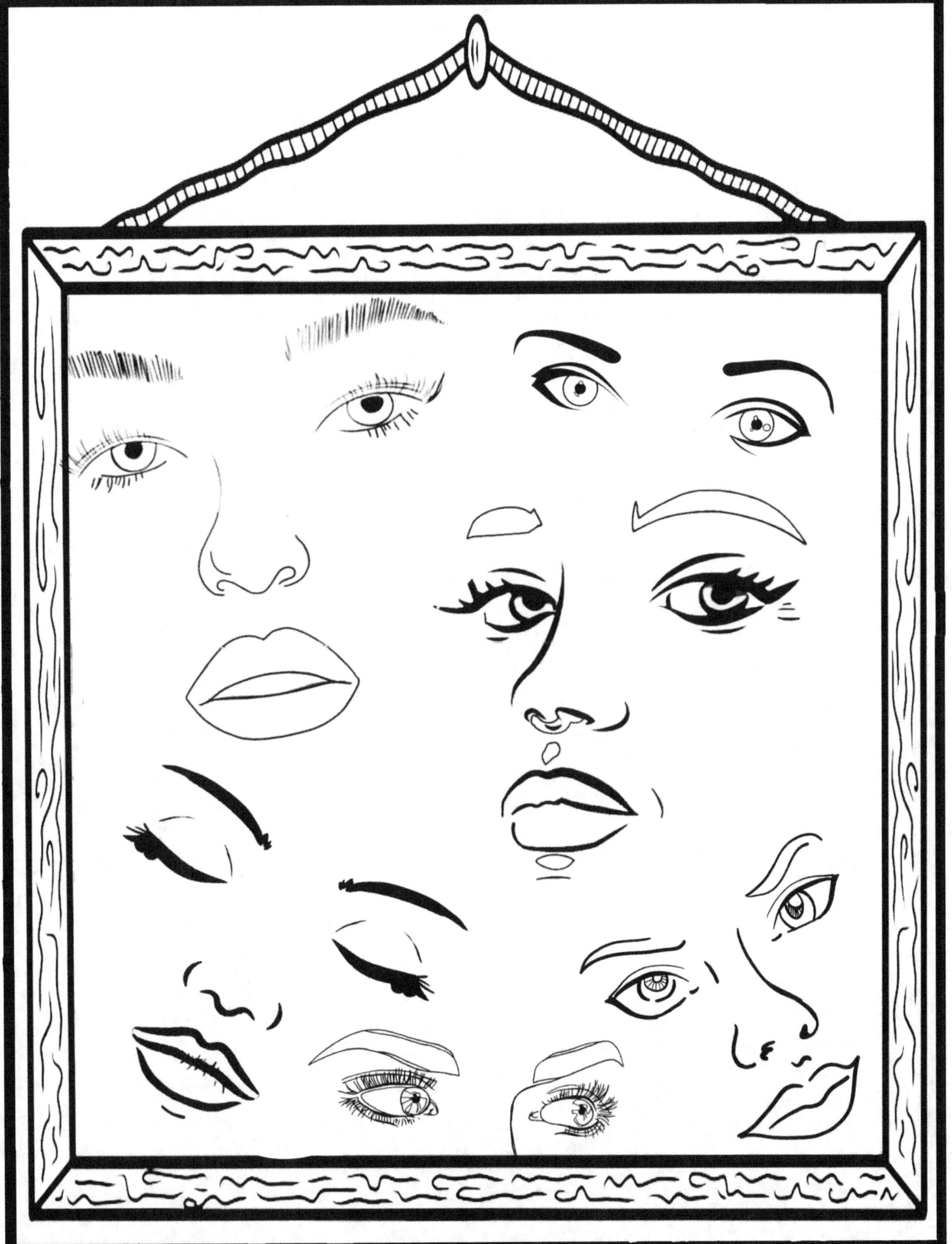

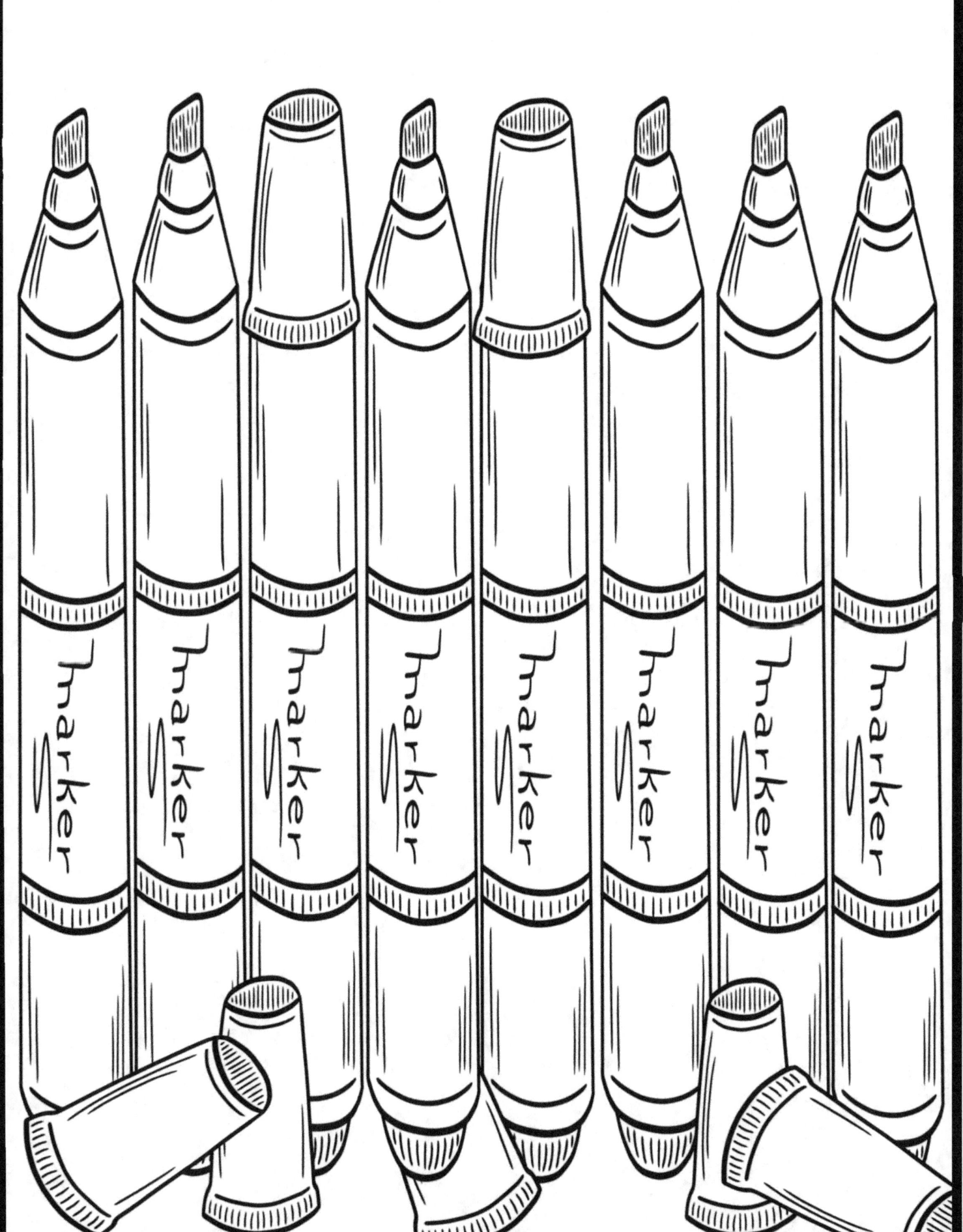

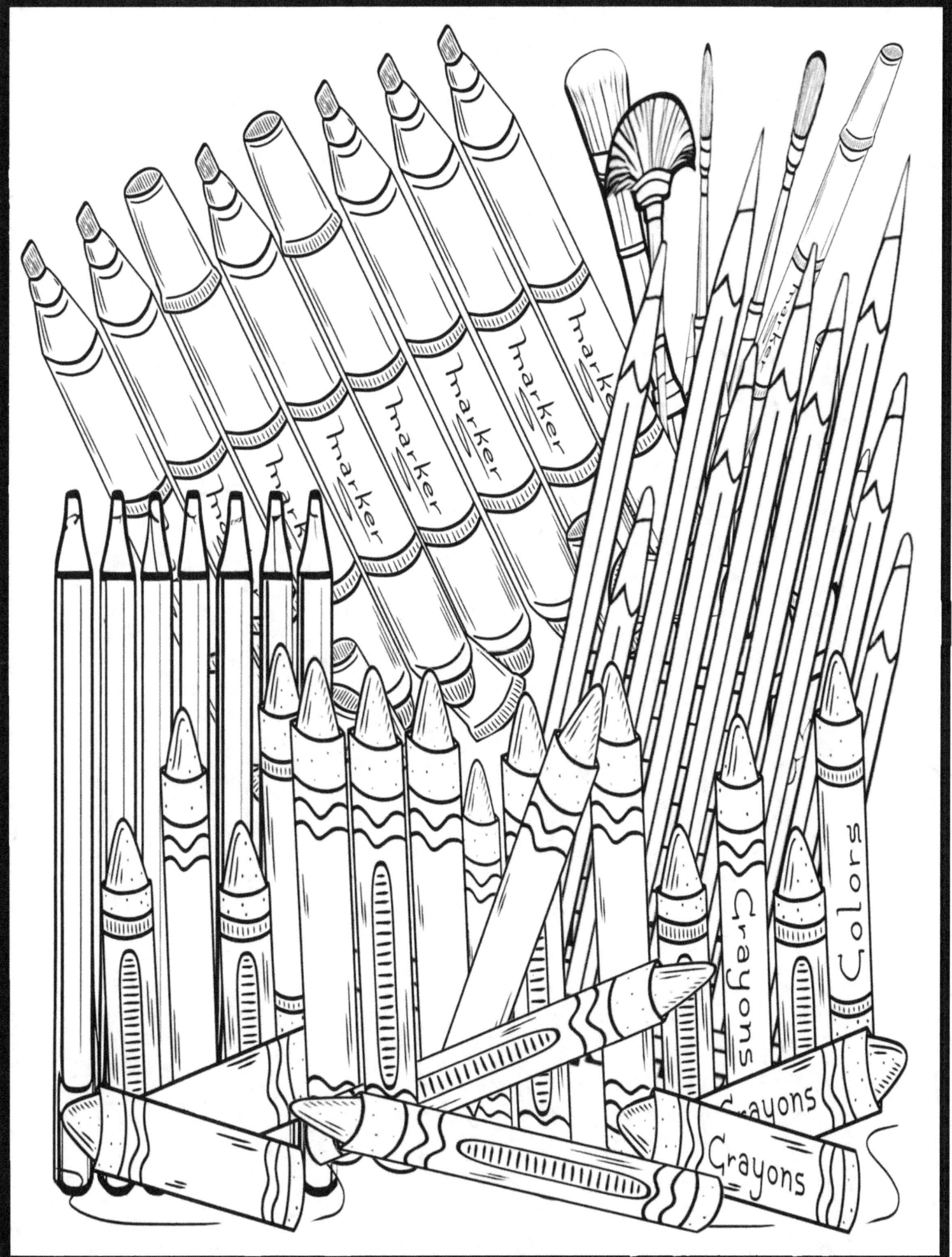

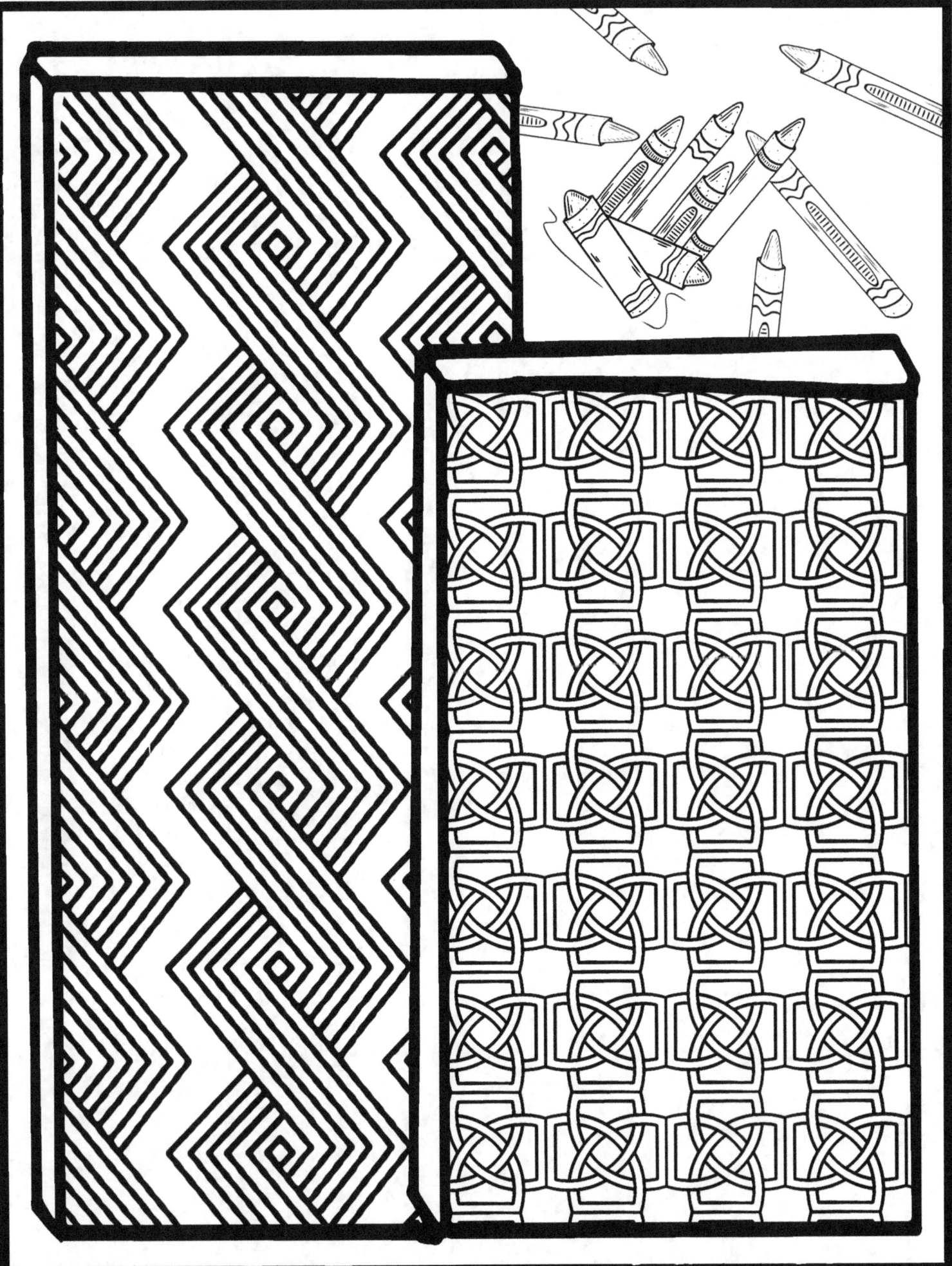

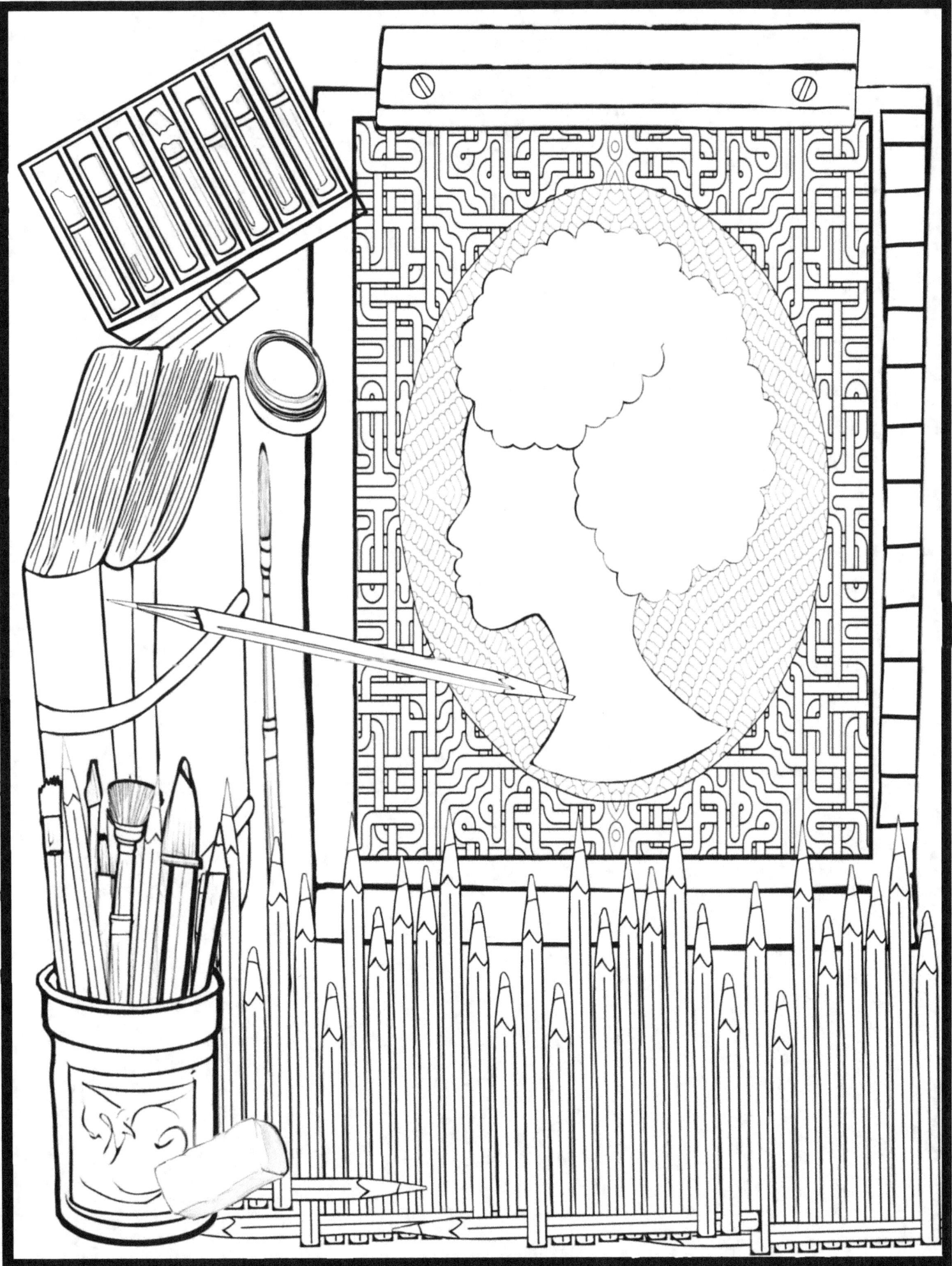

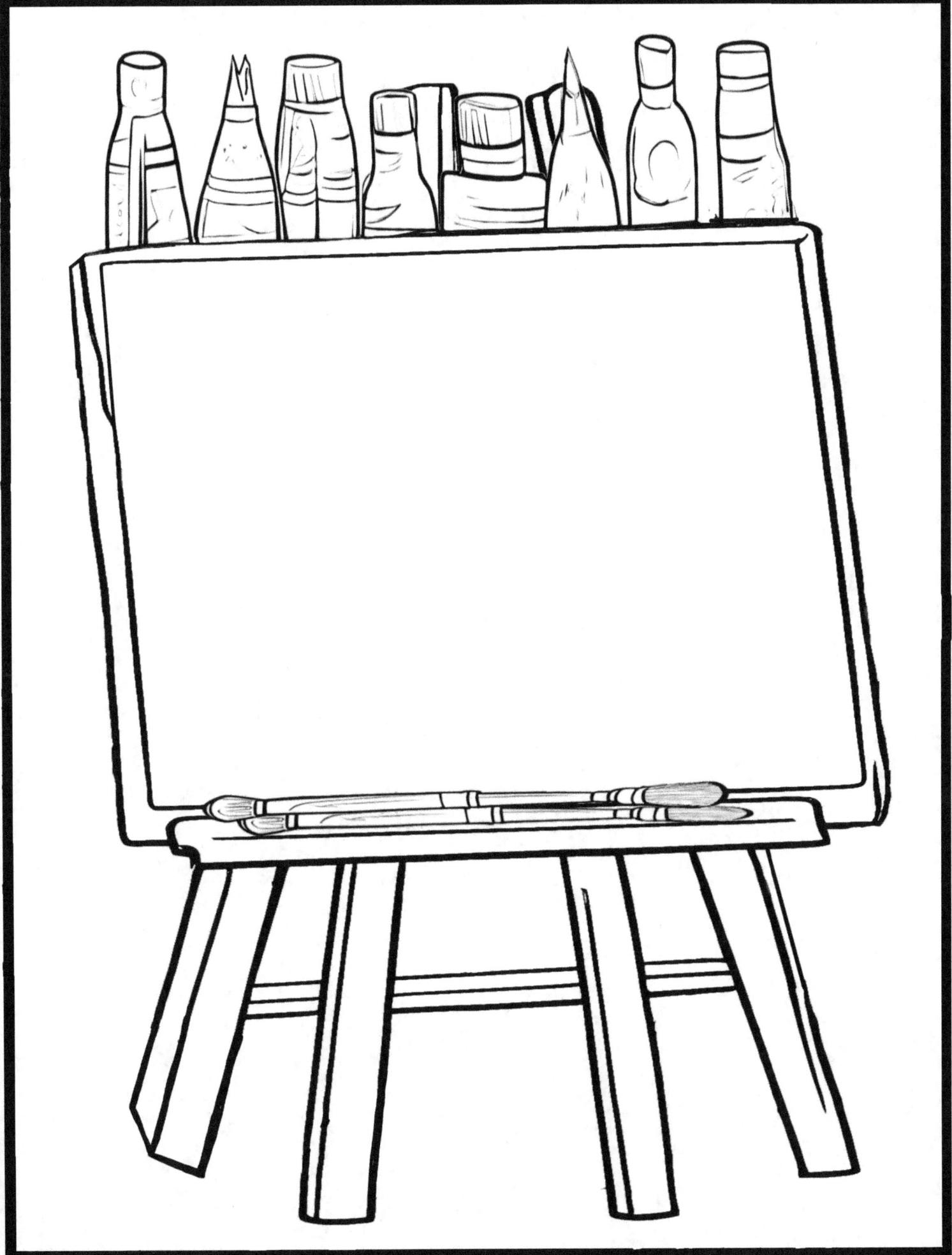

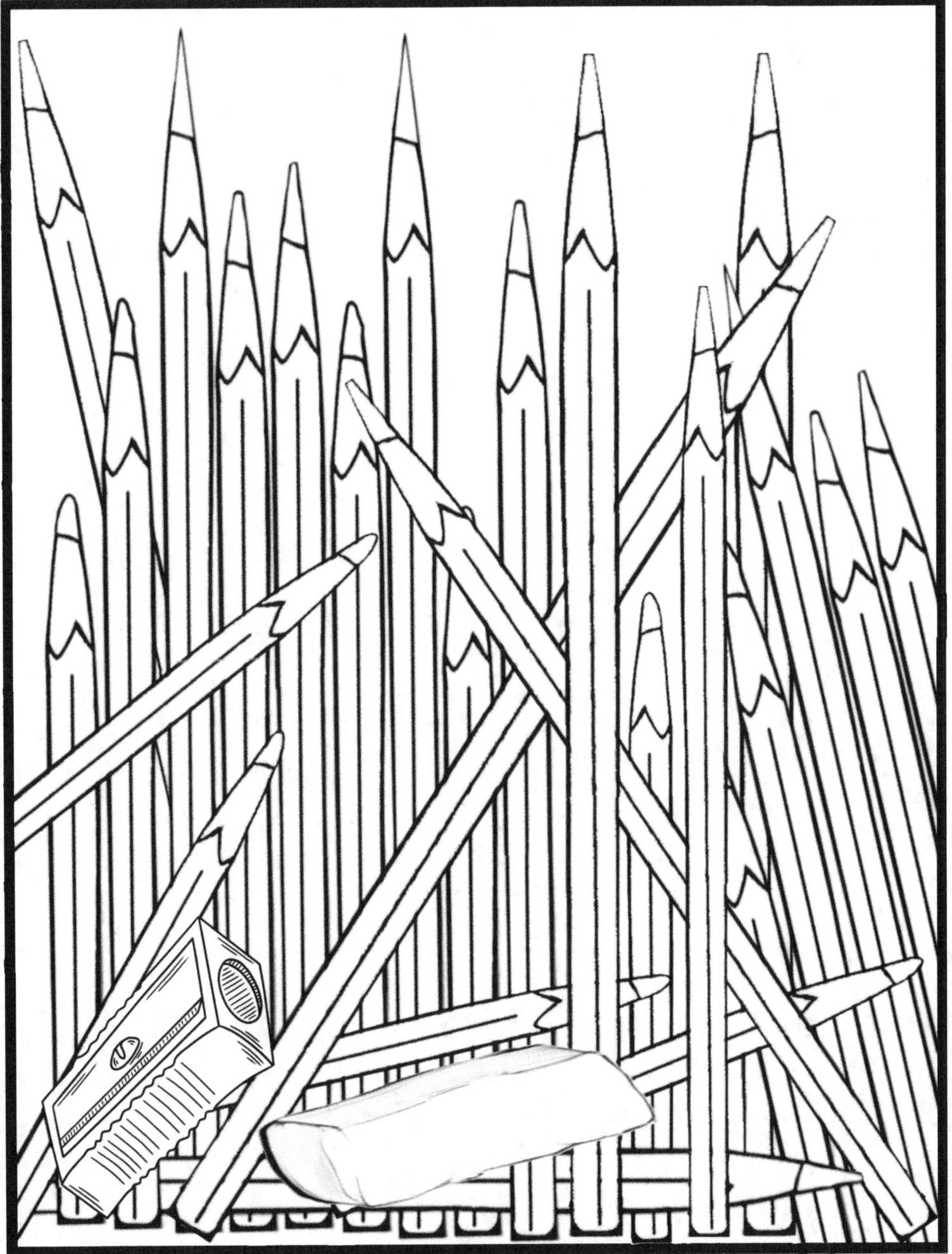

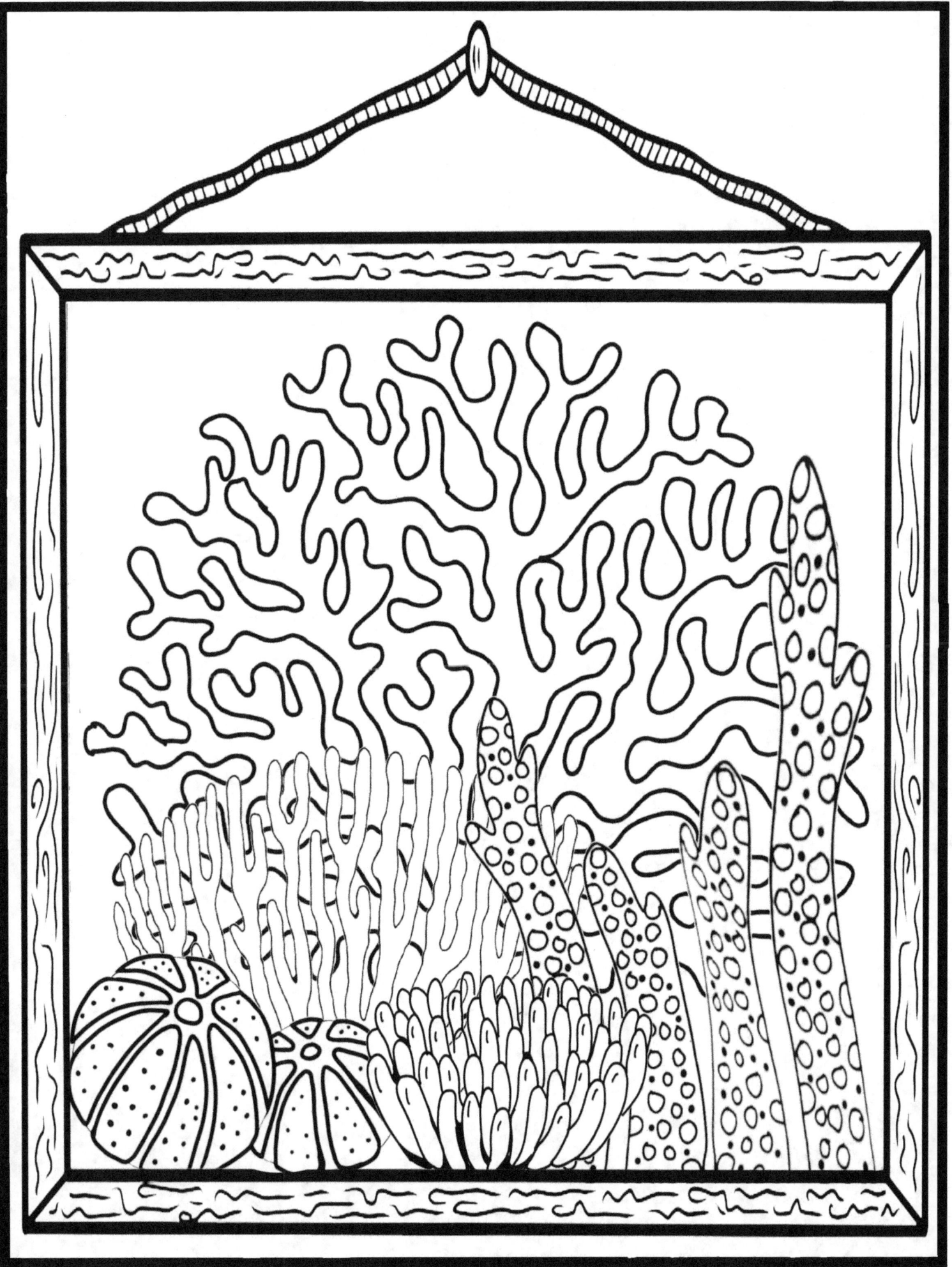

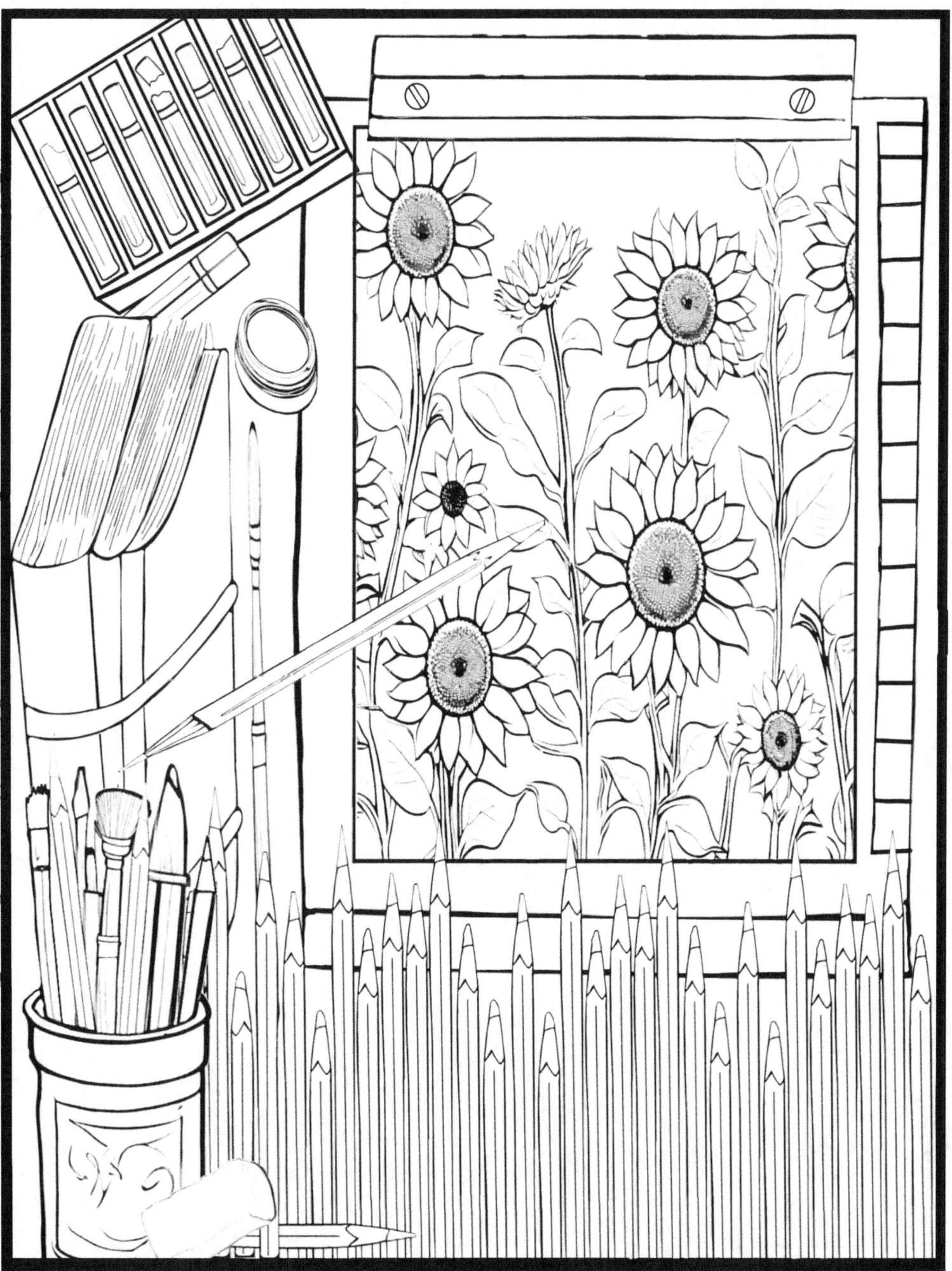

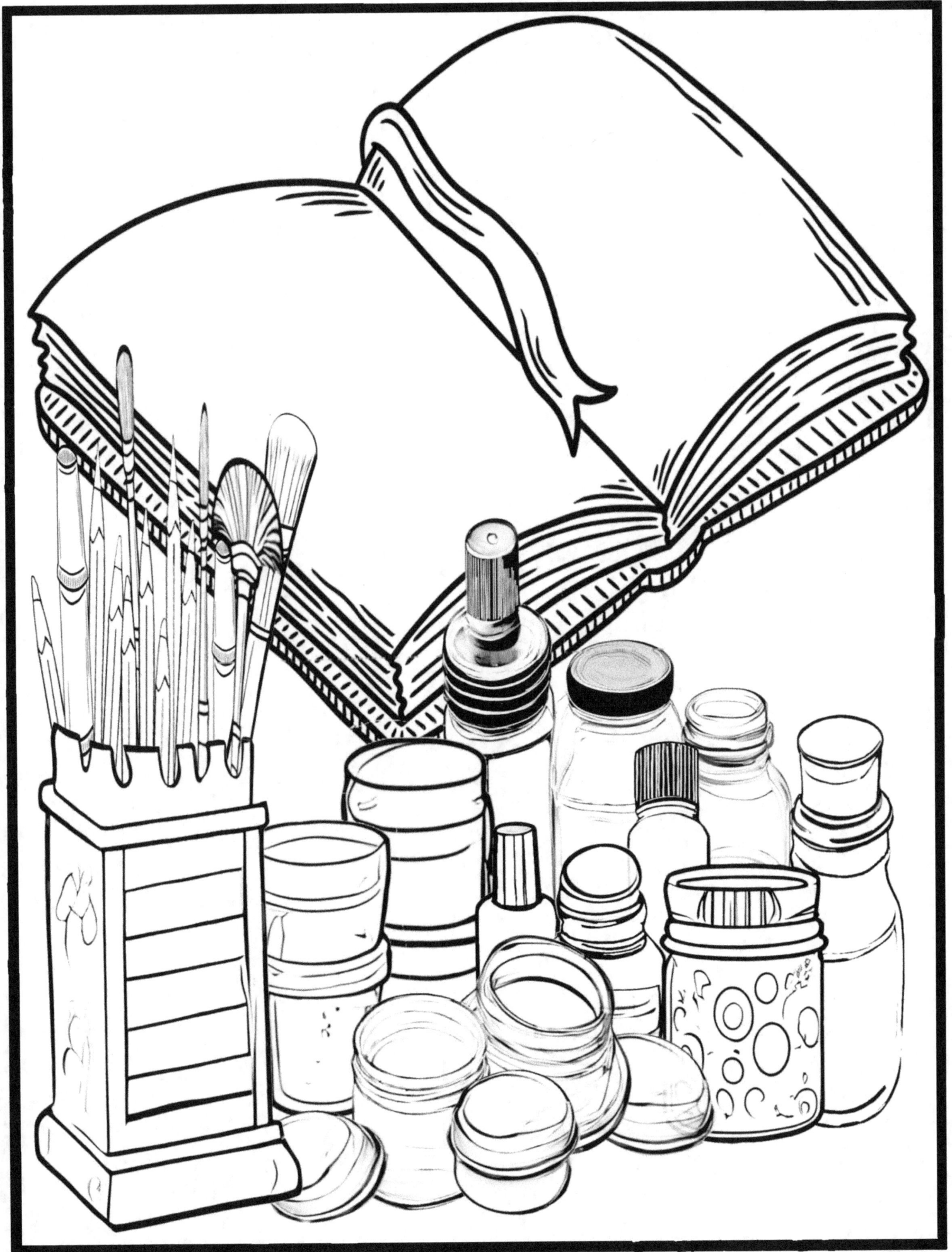

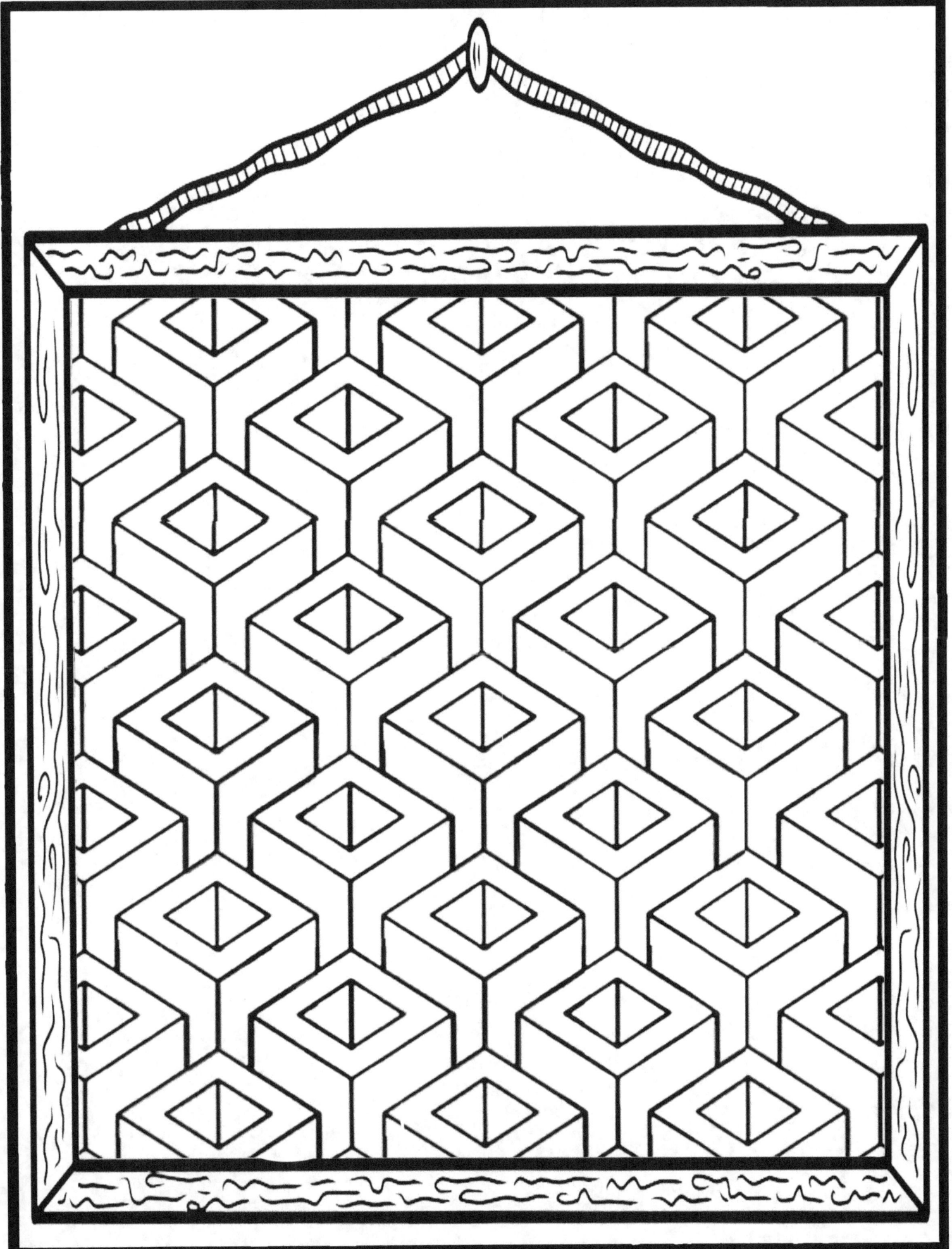

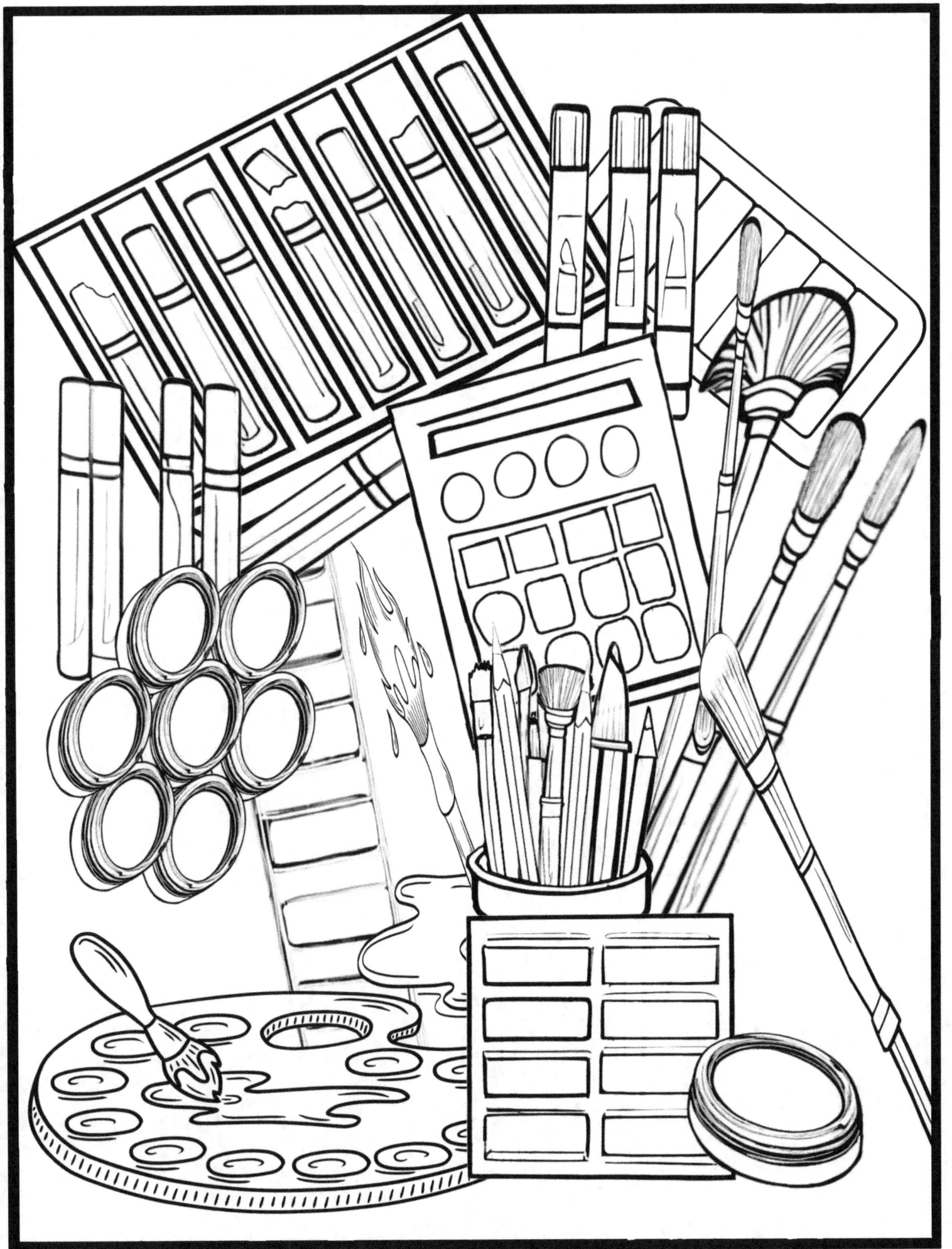

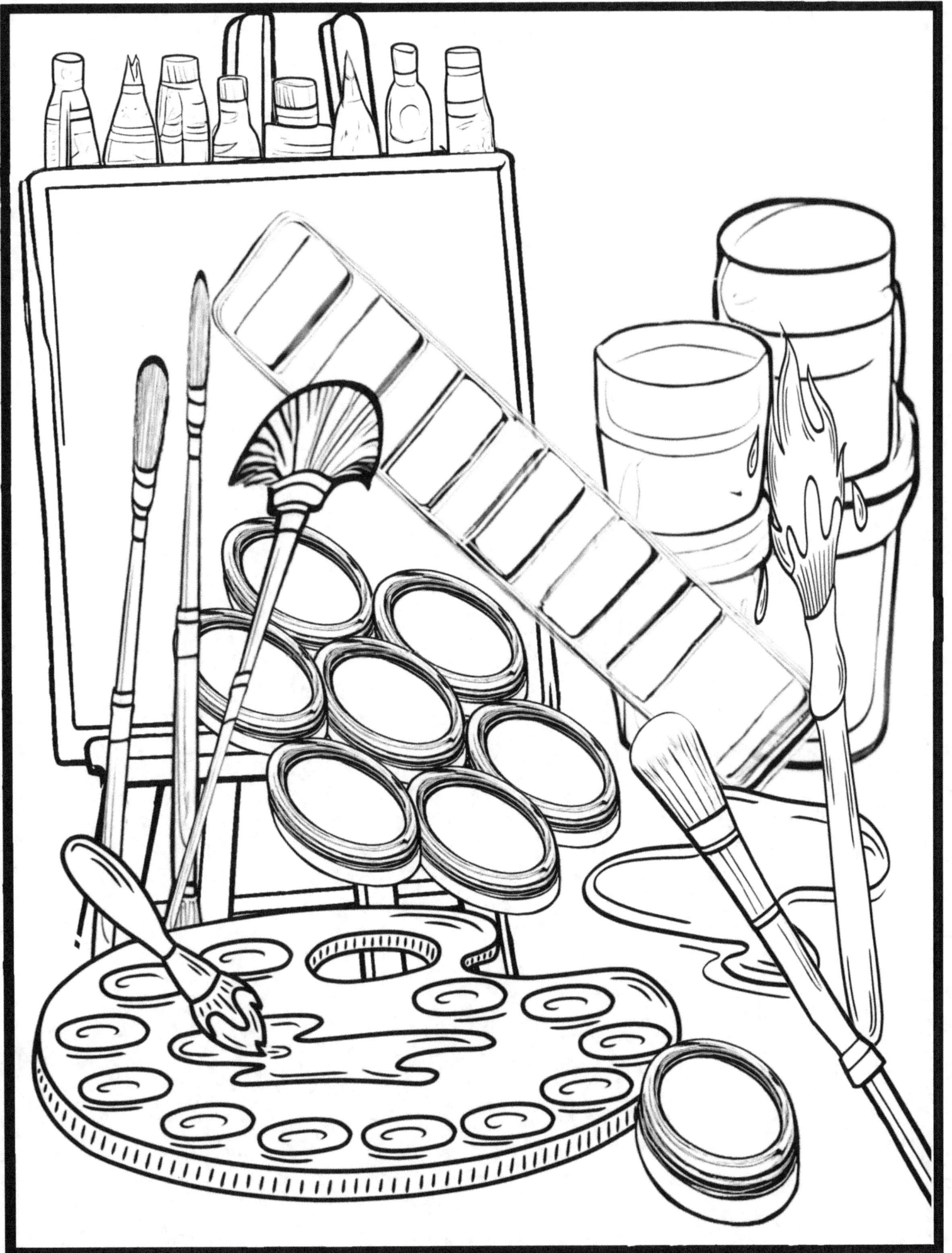

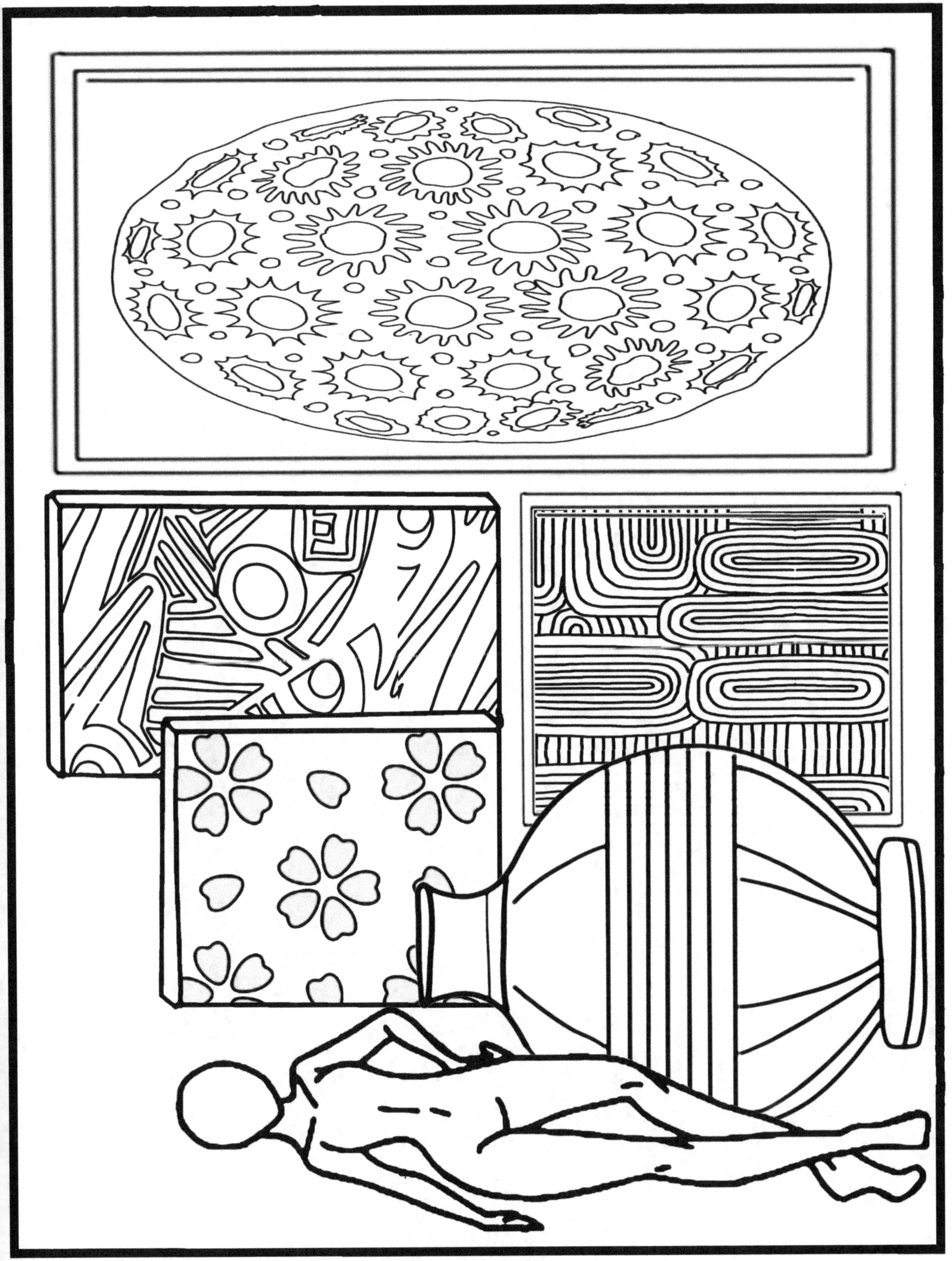

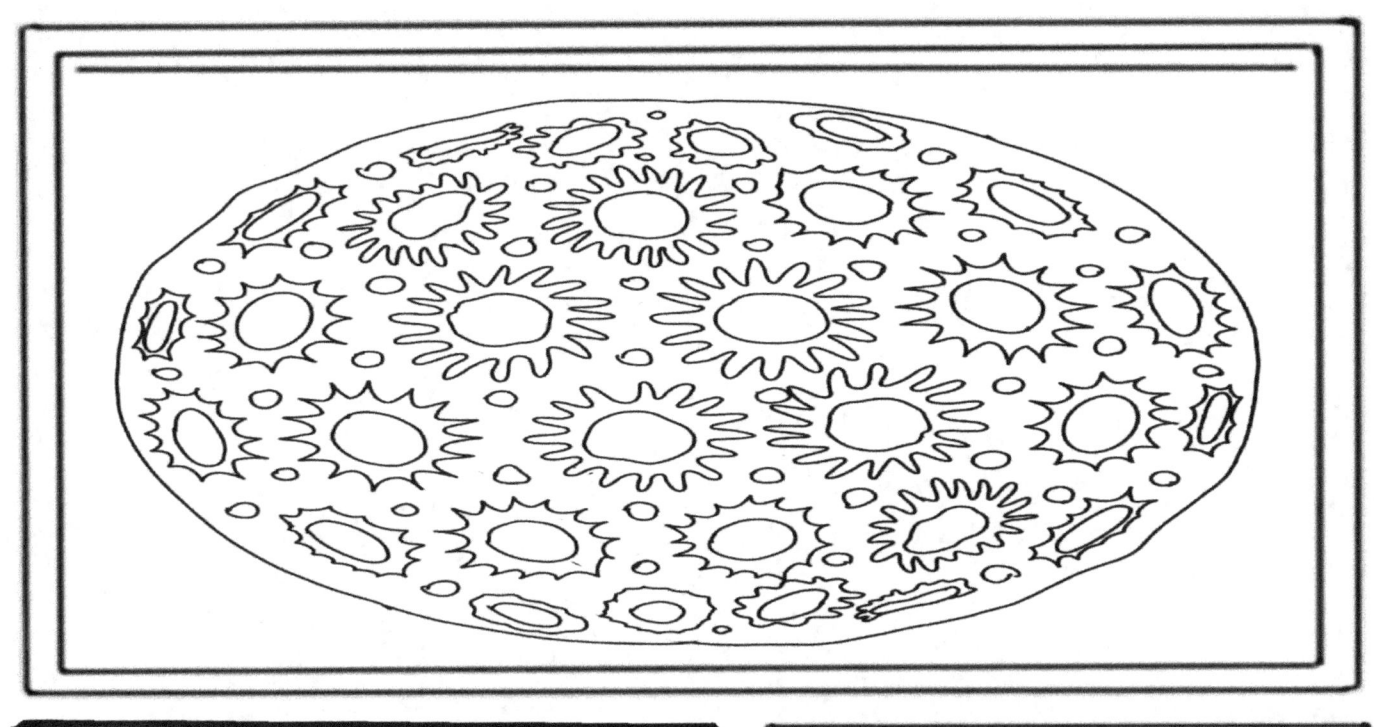

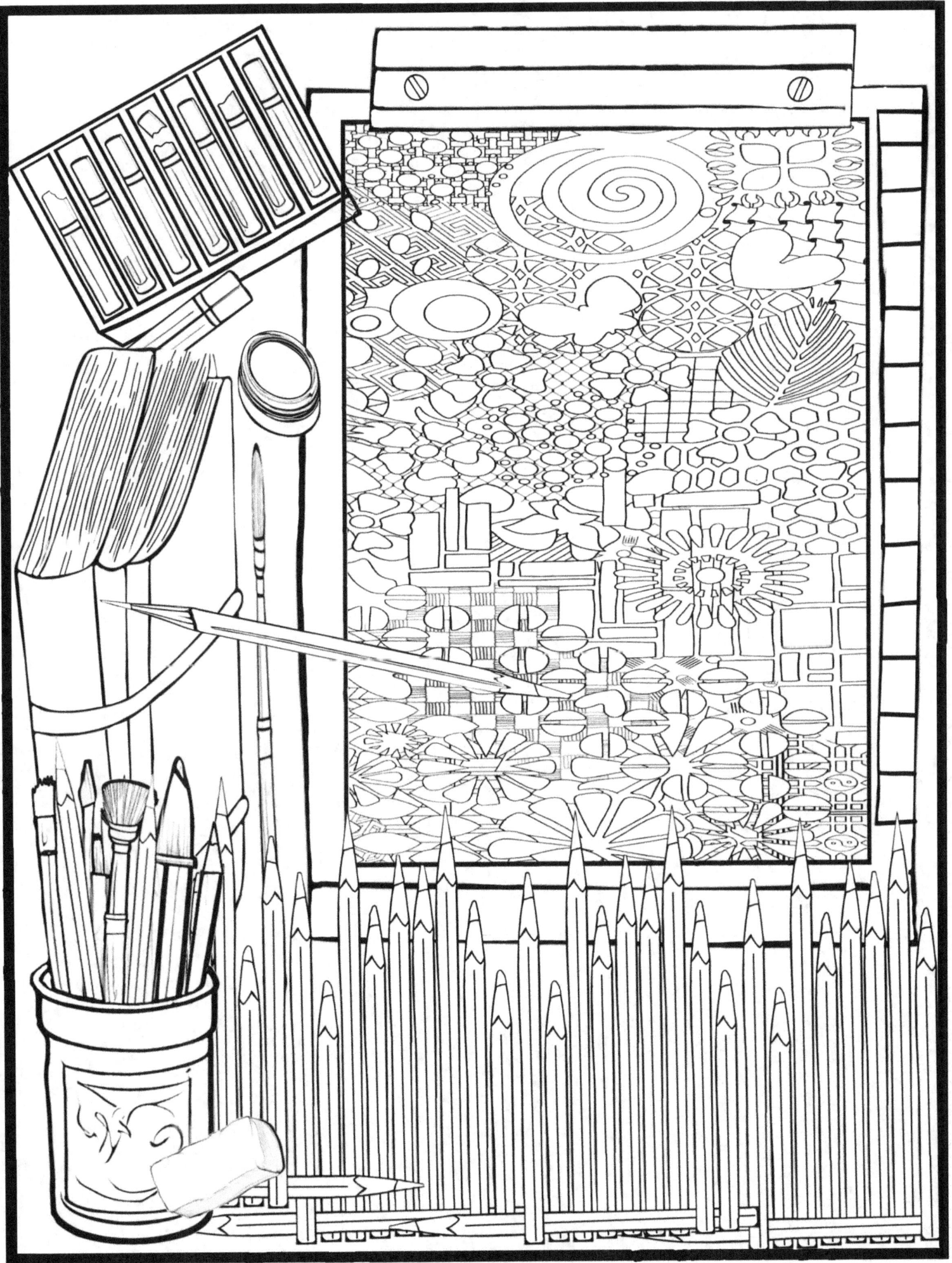

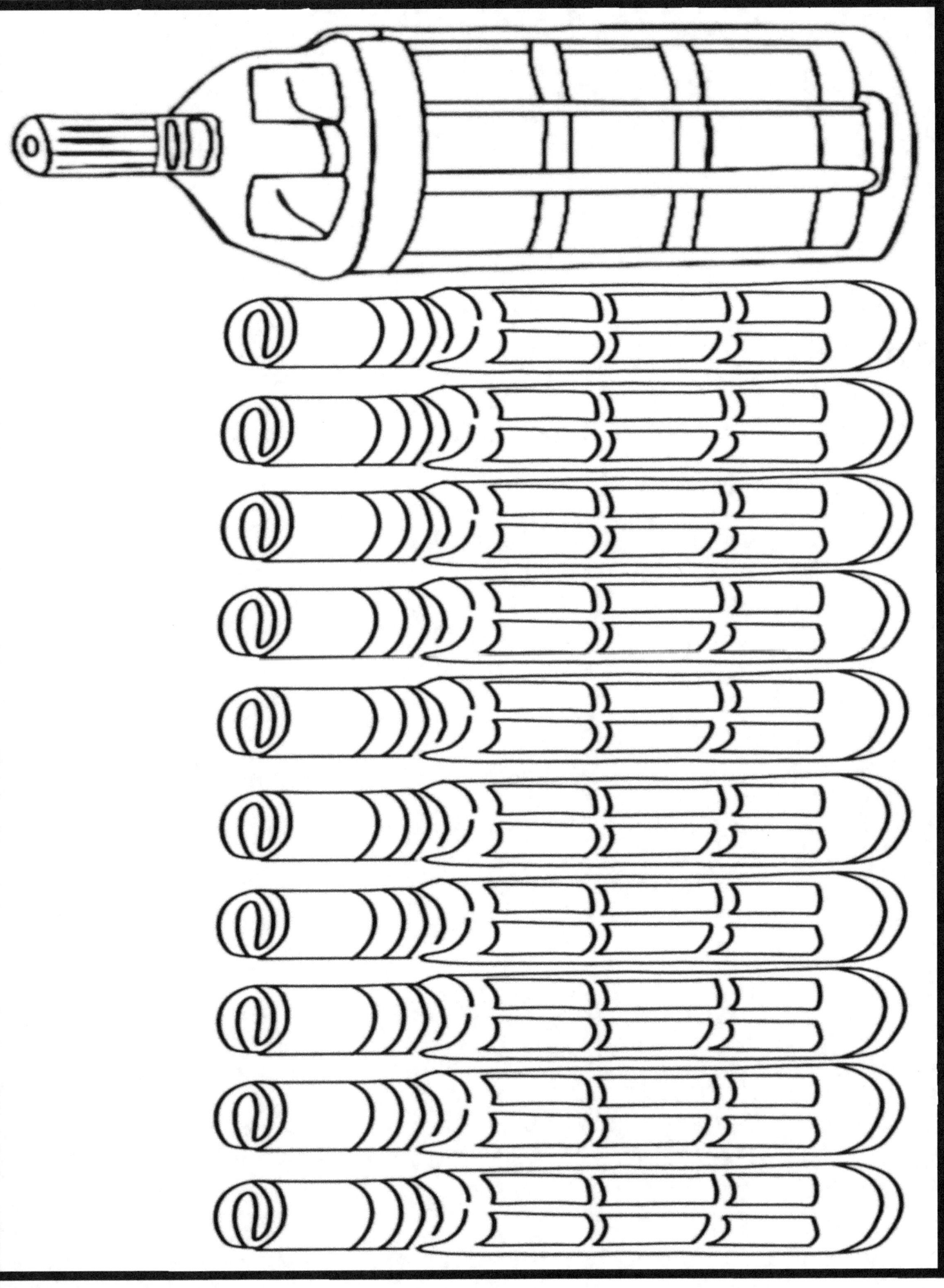

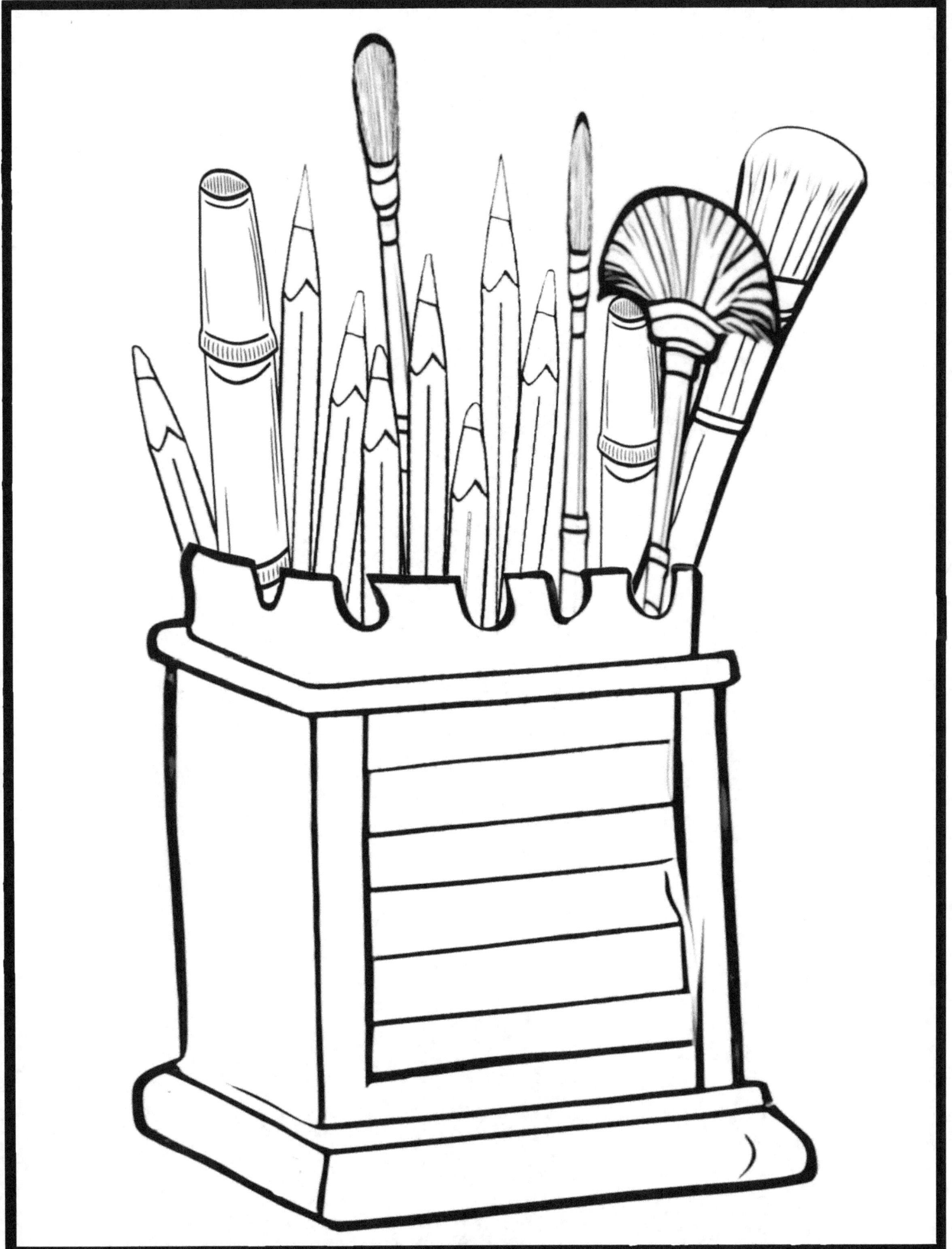

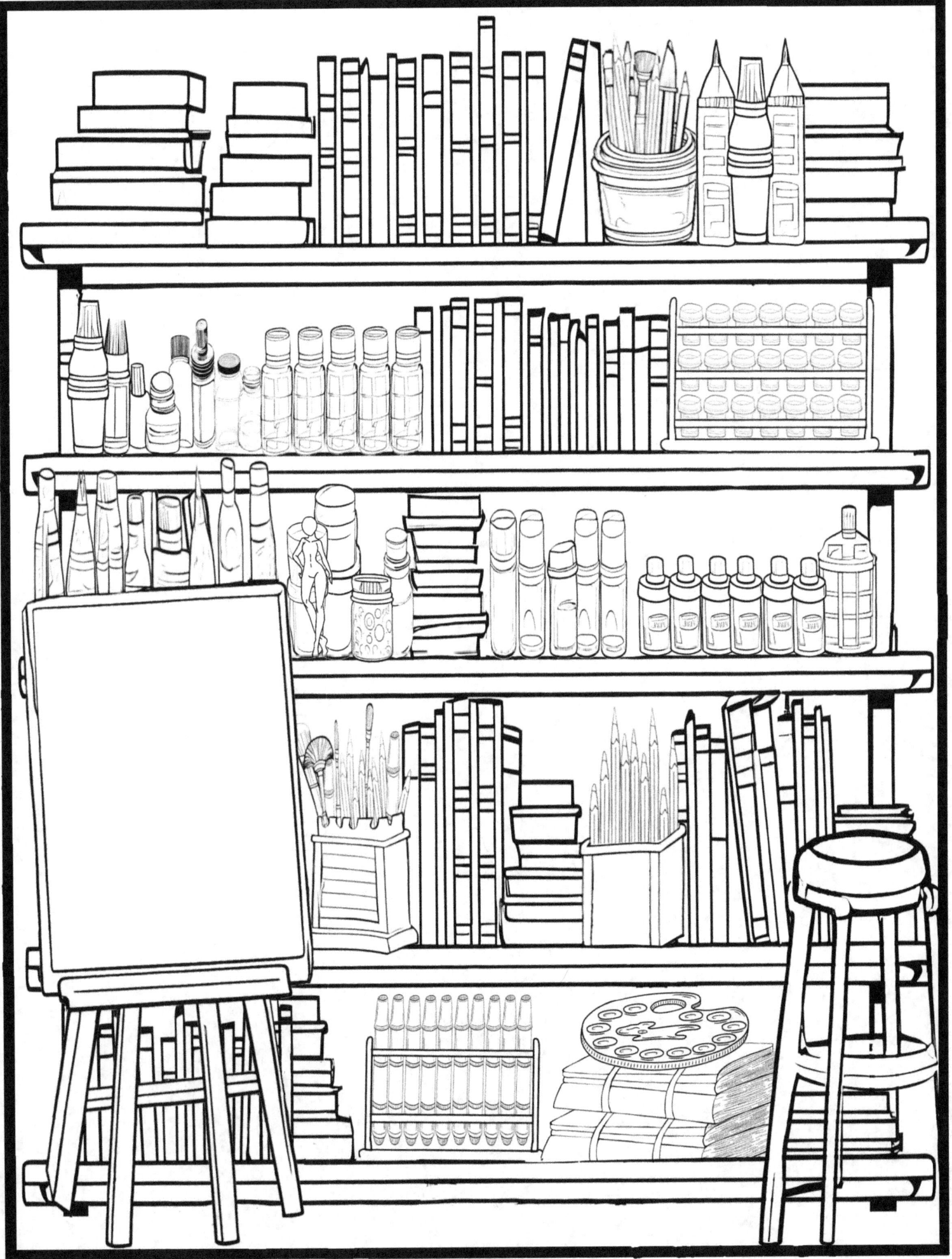

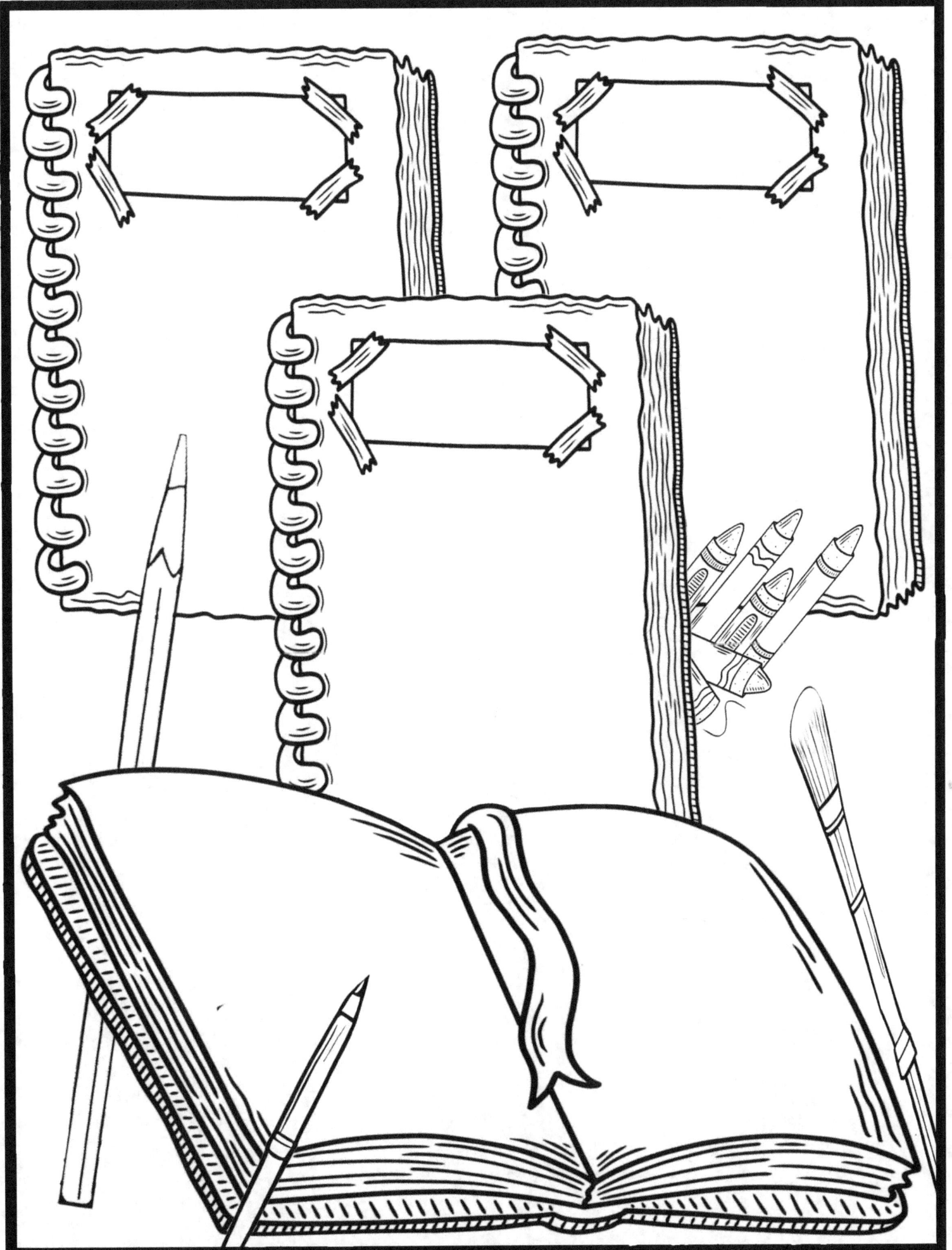

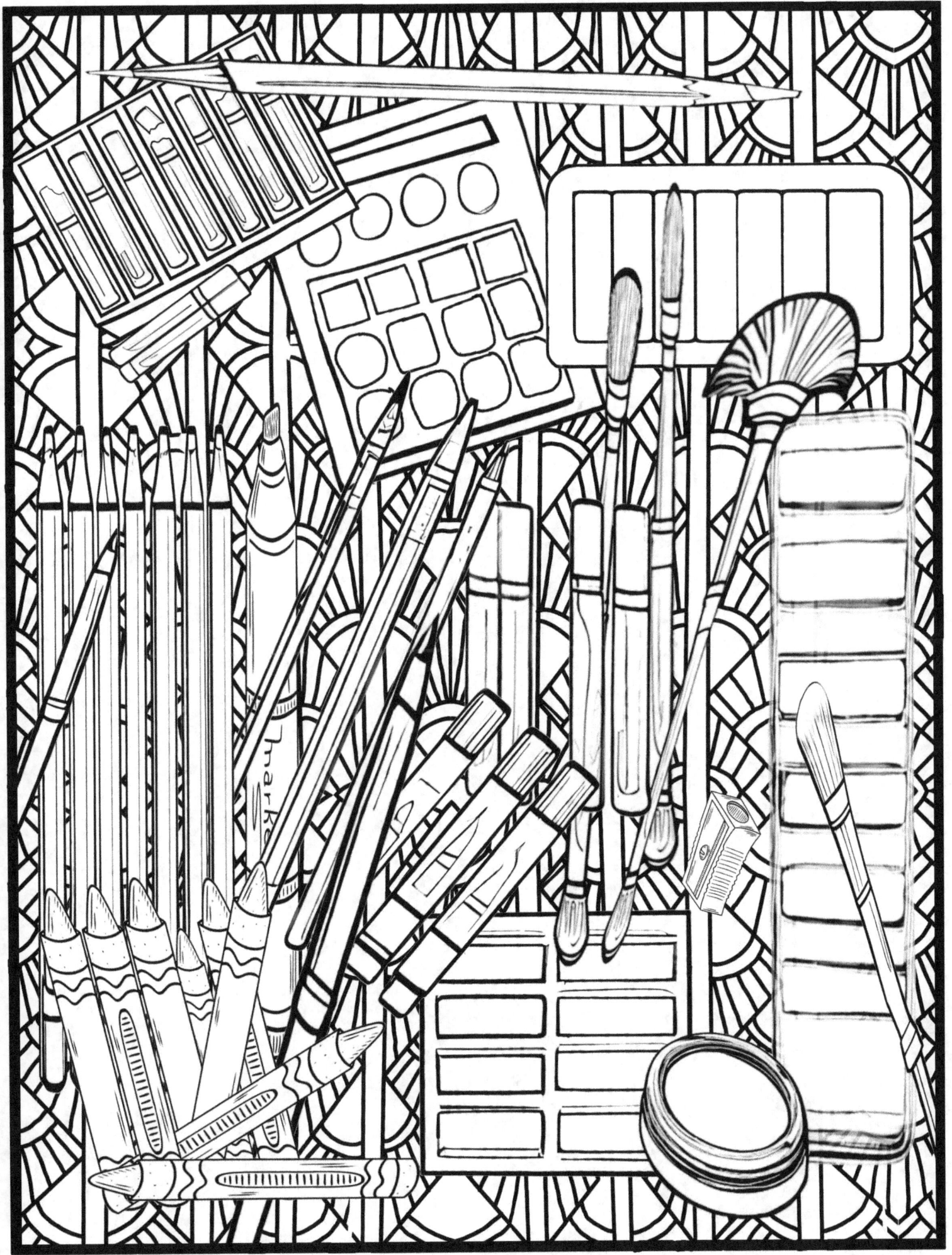

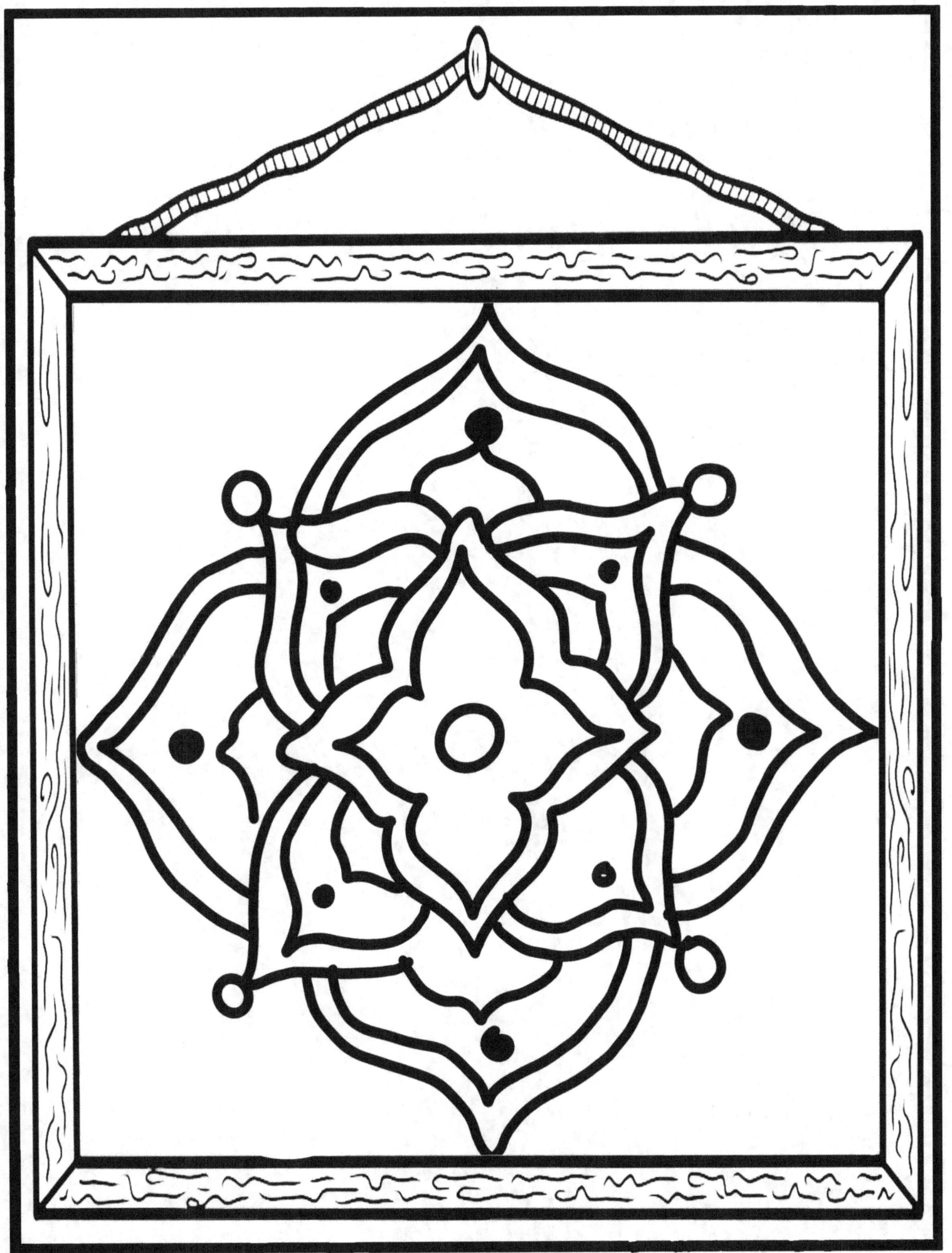

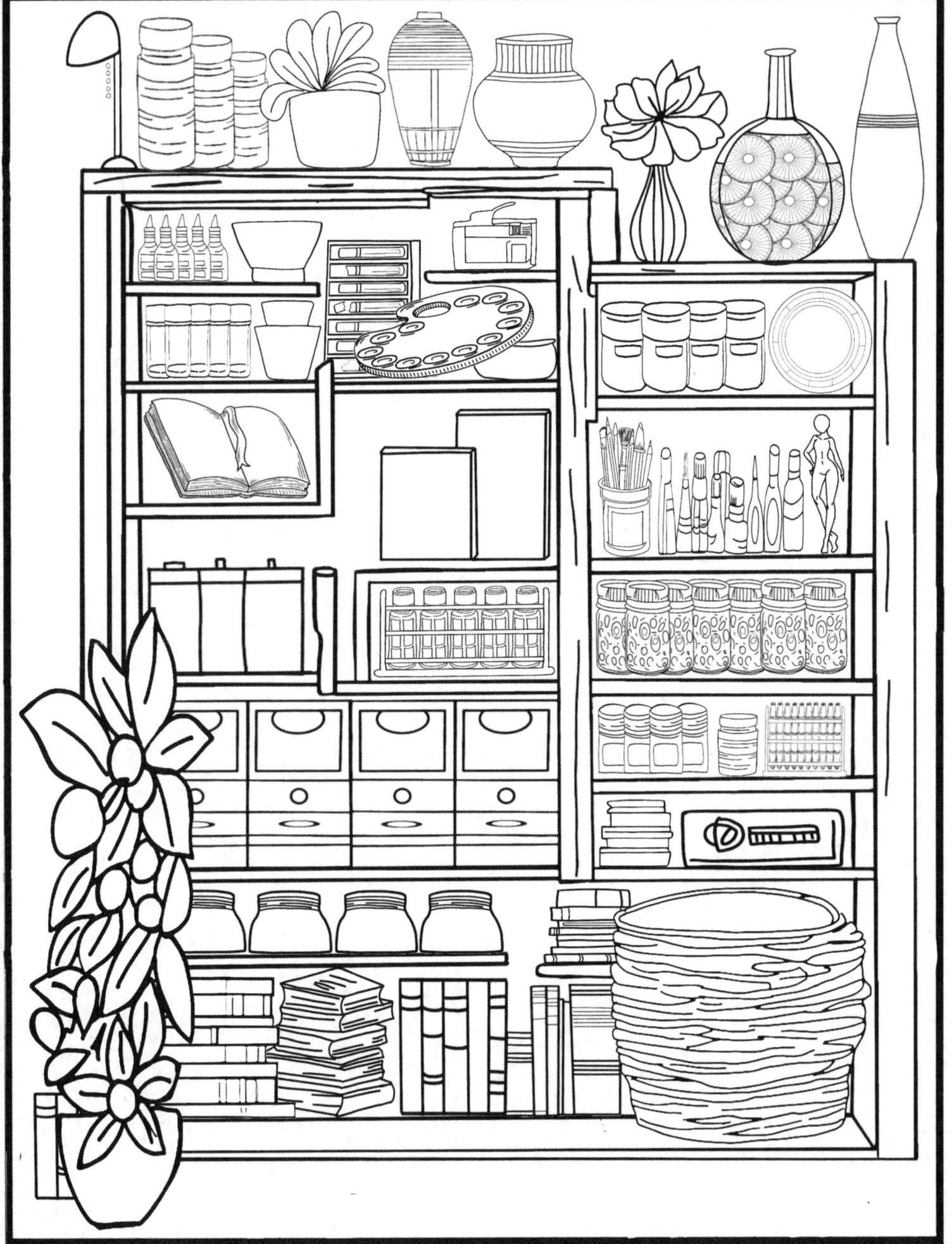

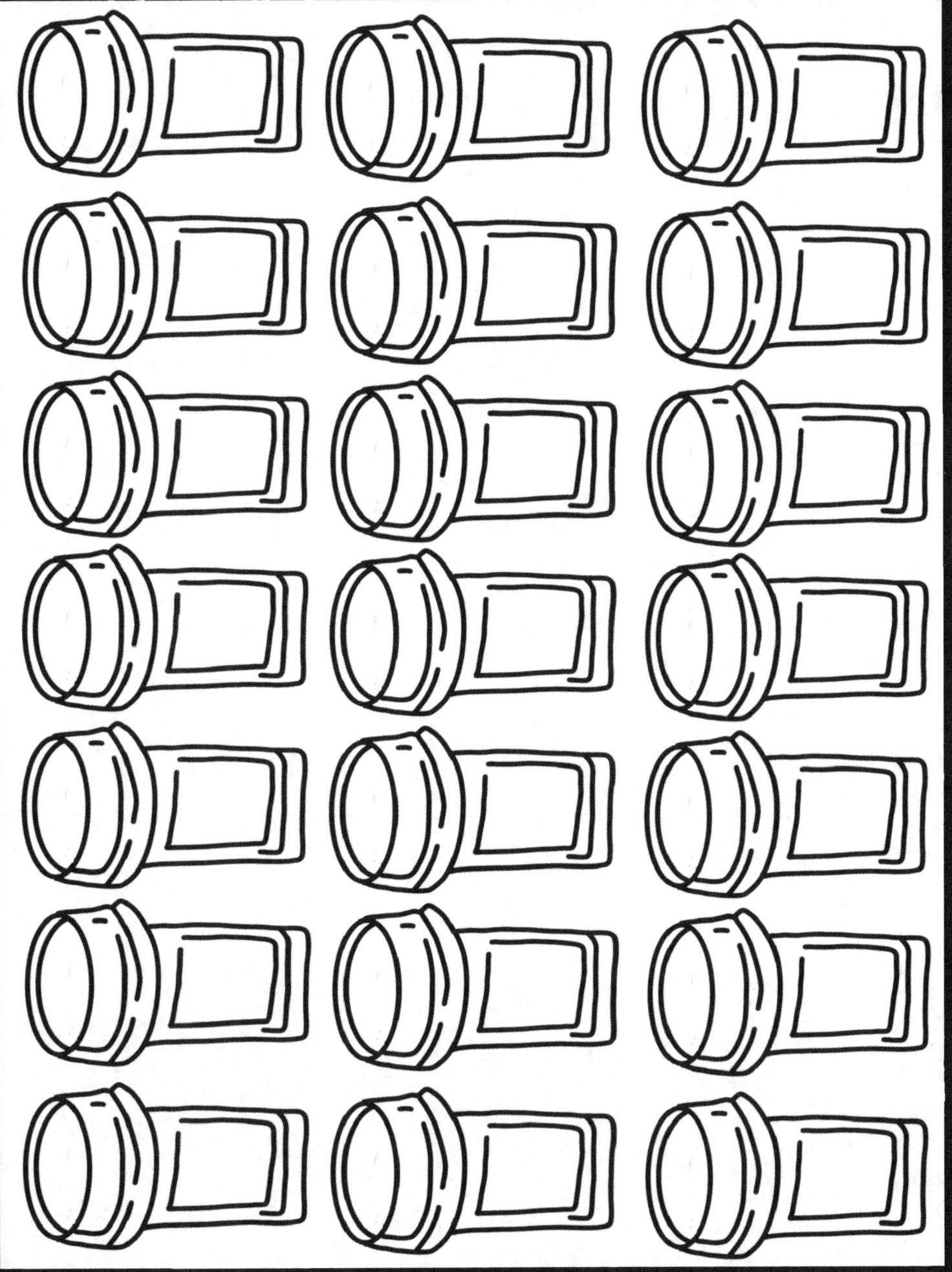

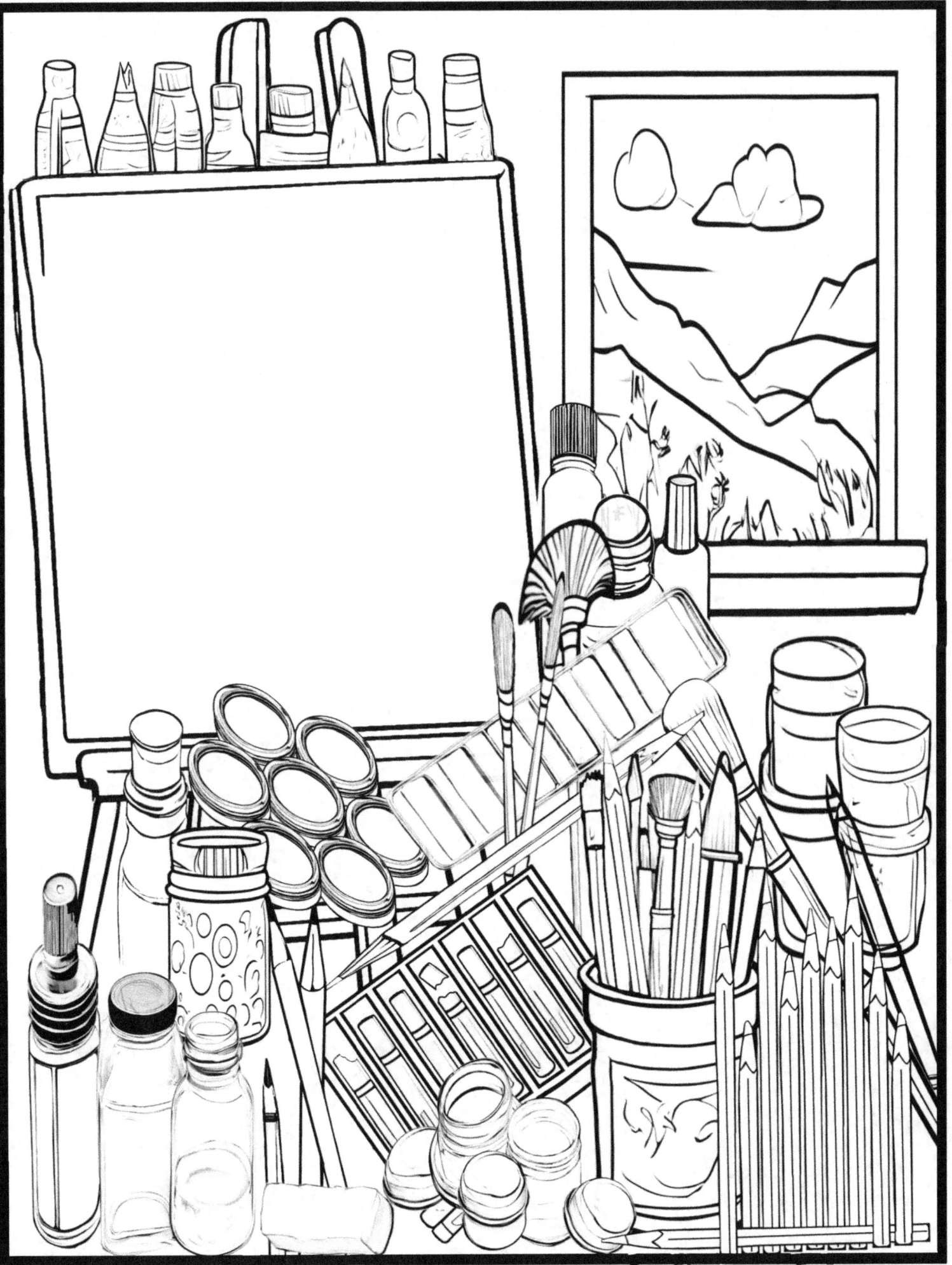

Chemwapuwa
Self-taught Artist
I started creating art under the name
Chemwapuwa, which is a South African
Zimbabwean name meaning "that which you
were given."

Yaimamess
Our mess is what we give to the world: we get
this mess from so many places throughout life.
If the mess you give & show to the world harms
no one, then celebrate that mess. It is beautiful.
Own your mess.

My Inspiration
LIFE

www.Yaimamess.com
Instagram.com/Yaimamess/

Namaste
Chemwapuwa

Test page

Test page

Test page

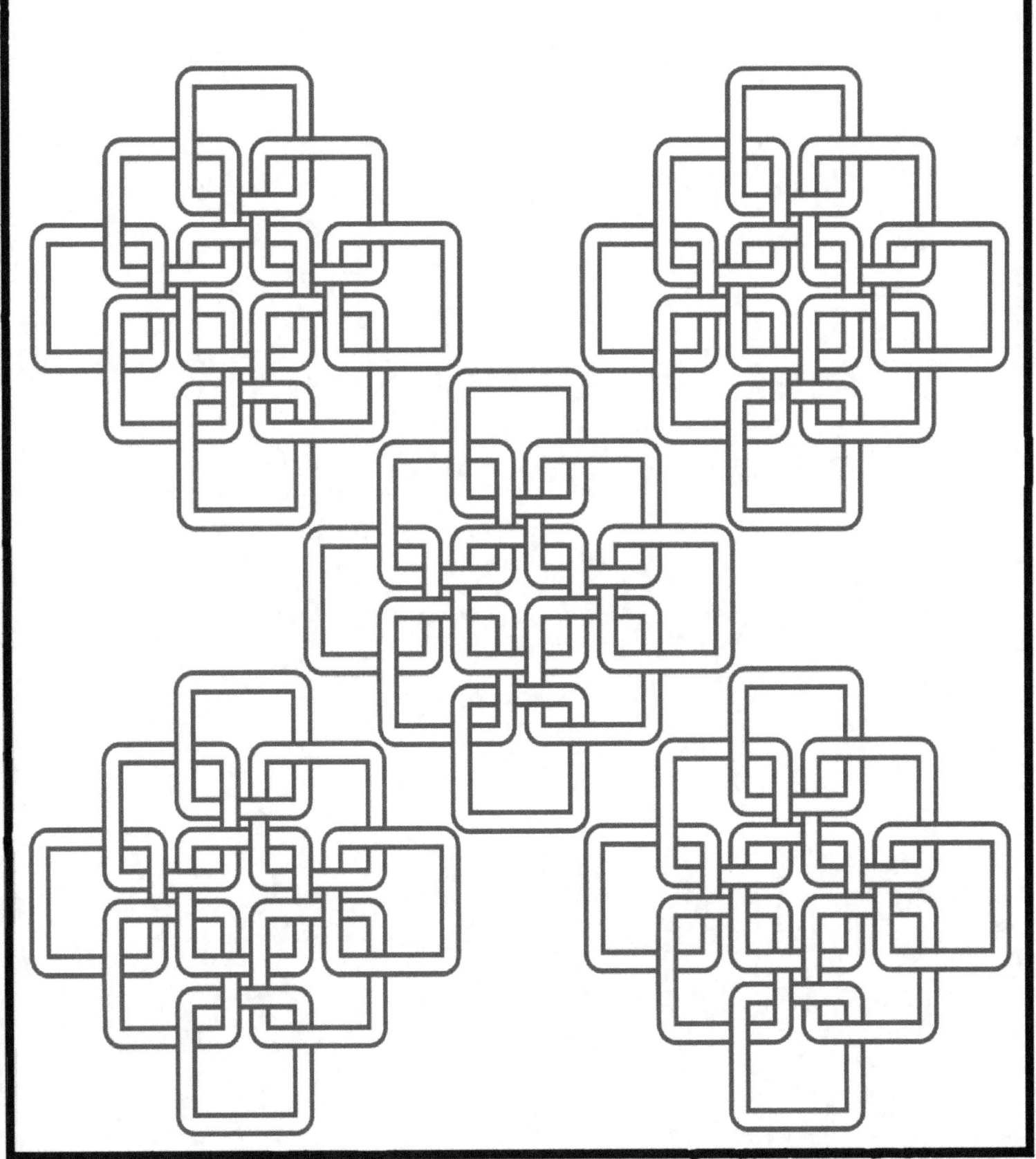

Enjoy this book try our other titles.

Calming Chaos: Geometric

Calming Chaos: ABC's & 123's

Calming Chaos: Angels

Calming Chaos: Foods

Calming Chaos: Steampunk

Calming Chaos: Celtic

Calming Chaos: Halloween 1st, 2nd, 3rd, & 4th

Calming Chaos: Home Sweet Home

Calming Chaos: Death

Calming Chaos: Love

Calming Chaos: Transport

Calming Chaos: Toys

and more